Advance pr

Custom Surveys Within Your Budget

"**Cooper and Philips have built a comprehensive guide for researchers and marketers.** This book will help employees minimize costs through the use of effective research strategies and tools."

John Andrews, former CEO, Giga Information Group, Inc.

"I need a resource that will help me build cost-effective online studies and this book does precisely that."

Garnor Morantes, Senior Manager, Ning, Inc.

"*Custom Surveys Within Your Budget* **allows researchers to focus their attention on helping the business improve.** It helps to minimize the time spent on the operational aspects of a research project and spend more time being an exceptional research consultant."

Neil Shah, Director of Research & Insights, Microsoft

"Research is a critical component to building a solid marketing strategy, yet all too often overlooked because it is thought to be too complicated, time consuming or costly. **Cooper and Philips have made custom research attainable by providing an indepth look at all aspects of research in a practical and easy to use format.** An invaluable research reference guide that every marketer should have in his or her arsenal."

Jim Umberger, President, Engage Marketing Group

"Cooper and Philip's comprehensive online research book explains the concept of research, how to execute strategies using specific methodologies, and helps define the direction needed to reach goals. **This book will become an invaluable resource to both marketers and researchers** and should elevate the importance of research to new heights."

Linda McLoof, former Executive Director,
News Research, ABC-TV

Practical Books for Smart Professionals from PMP

Order copies of **Custom Surveys Within Your Budget** for your entire research team. It will help them introduce new solutions to your existing operations and open the doors for new business development. You may also want to distribute the book to potential customers to engage them in the design and innovation of new research services and help them understand the power of online survey tools.

A customized edition, with *"Compliments of* **Your Company Name"** on the cover is available with orders of 200 or more copies. Call us toll-free at **888-787-8100** for quotes on quantity orders.

For more practical books for smart professionals, go to our website, **www.paramountbooks.com**.

Custom Surveys
Within Your Budget

Maximizing Profits
Through Effective Online
Research Design

Brian Cooper and Maria Philips

Paramount Market Publishing, Inc.

Paramount Market Publishing, Inc.
950 Danby Road, Suite 136
Ithaca, NY 14850
www.paramountbooks.com
Telephone: 607-275-8100; 888-787-8100   Facsimile: 607-275-8101

Publisher: James Madden
Editorial Director: Doris Walsh

Cataloging in Publication Data available
ISBN 13: 978-0-9819869-3-7 | ISBN 10: 0-9819869-3-5

Contents

Preface

Anyone who has spent years conducting market research will tell you that the one constant in Internet surveys is that nothing is ever constant. Researchers are always evaluating alternative approaches and must determine which solution will best solve the business requirements. Research is full of trade-offs. Market research is founded on scientific principles, but the decision-making process is subjective. Financial limitations, business requirements, or technology limitations may require an experienced researcher to make sacrifices to the study goals and objectives. To effectively manage the trade-offs, it is important not only to have a solid understanding of common research methods used today and the limitation of those methods, but also to understand how the specific implementations will affect survey outcomes online.

Limited budgets force marketers to rethink their research strategies and be realistic about their business needs. Understanding the different forces and making an acceptable decision is fundamental to a successful research project. The information contained within this book will help researchers and marketers understand the trade-offs so that they can make the best possible decision. Internet research is as much an art as it is a science. It's pliable and flexible, but most importantly it is effective and often the least expensive method to address customer needs and better understand a target market.

This book is a researcher's guide to executing online studies at all levels in a cost-effective manner. It is intended for use by researchers and business marketers who actively conduct or are planning to conduct market research surveys on the Internet. Readers should be able to look at the table of contents and quickly locate the specific issue with which they are dealing. *Custom Surveys Within Your Budget* is divided into distinct topic areas with clear subheads to easily identify a specific issue. The goal is to allow researchers and business marketers to quickly identify the area of interest to obtain an accurate solution. It begins with a basic understanding of Internet research, then focuses on general Internet research issues, and finishes with specific nuances of Internet research.

Acknowledgements

To my wife Carmen, thank you very much for the encouragement and standing by me. Mom and Dad, thank you for always supporting me. This one is for you Blake!

BRIAN COOPER

Thanks to my kids, Kenneth and Ian, and my mom, Millie, for being so supportive. A special thanks to my husband, Andy Duncan, for believing in me and giving me the gift of time to work on this project.

MARIA PHILIPS

Chapter 1

The Background of Internet Research

Although the market research industry is well developed, using the Internet for market research is relatively new. Nonetheless, researchers can learn a great deal from advances market research has made in other mediums of communication. The principles of research date back to the early 1800s with the advent of the standard deviation (Karl Pearson). One of the most important advances in research was the invention of the Likert scale (e.g., *Do you Strongly Disagree, Disagree, Neither Agree/Disagree, or Agree or Strongly Agree?*). Although this may seem basic now, its construct has been used over thousands of surveys for the last 80 years. Focus groups were invented in the 1940s and Gallup's impact on the Truman election gave researchers initial insight into how to properly conduct research. Quantitative and qualitative research evolved through the decades and in the late 1990s online survey research became prominent.

The benefits of online research were quickly realized: cost savings, ability to collect more completes in a shorter period of time, and ability to show visual images. In addition, Internet access was becoming widespread, creating the ability to reach respondents through email. New companies surfaced with innovative technological tools as the traditional offline research tools used for telephone or mail research rarely worked well in online studies.

Technology allows companies to reduce costs by minimizing or eliminating the use of telephone interviewers, which limits the number of respondents that can be contacted at one time. Telephone interviews are also slower because the interviewers must read the questionnaire to the respondent and record the responses. Lengthy tabulation decks are no longer necessary because the data is stored online. In addition, there have been improvements in management efficiencies because data analysis and calculations can be made directly using tools embedded in the program. In many cases, these tools shorten the length of time it takes to conduct a survey and publish results, allowing a company to make quicker decisions. Today, some research companies even promote their technology tool as the primary differentiator that makes them more successful compared with other such companies. The trick is to harness the technology, which we'll discuss in depth in this book.

New developments in Internet research

A drawback of this new technology is that it is not fully developed. There are still quite a few kinks to be resolved that can be especially important with complex ad hoc or tracking, or customer satisfaction studies. If the respondent base is largely unavailable on the web, then obviously this medium of communication will not work. New strategies and approaches are developed on the fly to accommodate the always-changing needs of clients, but sometimes at a hefty expense. In many situations, complex surveys require custom software development. For example, a client may want a product concept test fully functioning inside of a survey tool before it has been fully tested. Unless the survey platform provider can be convinced that the new development is good for all of its customers, or if the client spends millions of dollars on numerous research projects with the provider, it is unlikely that the research provider will pay for the development.

The process innovations developed today for online surveys are different from the older telephone-based surveys. Online survey programs generally have "point and click" functionality to create a questionnaire. This allows project managers to quickly get up to speed on a survey software program and begin creating and implementing surveys on their own in a matter of weeks. Older phone surveys required those creating the survey to be fluent in complicated programming logic, much like a computer software developer uses to create code for a website.

In addition, the online interface has advanced. With telephone interviews, it did not matter what the survey interface looked like because the respondent never saw it. However, with online surveys, it is especially important that the interface is easily navigable and clear because the questionnaires are self-administered. There is no interviewer verbally explaining the survey to the respondent. Thus, the online research programs developed today have to serve two fundamental purposes: First, to provide a user-friendly graphical interface for respondents to see and second, to incorporate an automated mechanism to capture, store, sort, and view responses to specific questions.

Comparisons with phone and mail survey technology

Comparing methodologies, phone surveys do not require the user-friendly, graphic element that online surveys do, so complex survey rules are written specifically for the phone interviewer. In addition, as part of the research process, telephone interviewers are briefed on the nuances of the survey prior to the launch of a study. In contrast, online survey rules must be programmed directly into the survey because it is self-administered.

Mail surveys do require a user-friendly interface, but they are not used if complex skip patterns and targeted questioning to a specific sub-segment of the sample are required. Mail surveys are also subject to more errors when a respondent does not follow directions correctly. For example, respondents completing a mail survey may check multiple answers when the instructions asked to check only one. These kinds of errors result in missing data, meaning the number of responses to the question would be fewer than the number of respondents asked the question. This can potentially lead to erroneous interpretation of the results.

A phone or web survey can prevent certain user errors from occurring. In the case of telephone interviews, the interviewer can repeat the question and clarify questions to some degree. Interviewers are trained to answer a respondent's questions without leading the respondent. Most online surveys have a help link at the bottom of the page to answer questions and the programming itself can eliminate errors. For example, if only one answer is required and the respondent checks off multiple responses, an error message would pop up instructing respondents on how to correct their answers.

There also appear to be some differences in how respondents answer online and telephone-based surveys. Online surveys typically generate a more robust set of responses. For example, if a "check all" question is used in both an Internet survey and a telephone-based survey, respondents are likely to select more responses online than in a telephone interview. This may be due to respondents forgetting all of the possible selections and only selecting the most critical responses they can recall, or possibly a sense of time pressure. In the case of online surveys, respondents can review the answer set multiple times and select as many responses as are appropriate.

Chapter 2

How to Determine if Your Study Should be Conducted Online

Internet surveys are often employed primarily to lower costs, but not all research studies should be conducted online. Cost reduction should never be the only criteria used to decide if a survey should be online.

The target audience for a survey is an important consideration in deciding whether it should be conducted online. The target audience must have access and preferably use the Internet on a regular basis. Until recently, senior citizens were generally not good candidates for an Internet survey because they were not as familiar with the Internet as younger groups. Young children that are not yet able to read and type would not be good candidates for online surveys because they would need to be coached through the questionnaire. When conducting business-to-business research, executive-level respondents may be difficult to recruit via email. Thus, a phone survey may be recommended for certain audiences.

Online surveys were initially conducted among technology workers because they were the first to have a large portion of their population with access to the Internet. Many companies were hesitant to use online research until recently because it was believed that not a large enough proportion of populations under investigation would be connected to the Internet. As long as the target population is connected, it is safe to say that an online survey can be conducted.

In research, answers are rarely a black and white. Because research is not a perfect science, answers are typically found through evaluating the different requirements, the pros and cons of an approach, objectively thinking about the impact on the business and research outcomes. In many cases, it is quite simple to determine if a study should be conducted online, but with certain research areas, it may be more difficult to determine the proper method.

To determine the ideal mode of communication for research, you can evaluate the trade-offs by grouping them in the following four buckets:

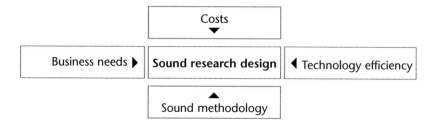

Business needs

Business needs are the most important consideration when undertaking market research. The business need drives the request for proposals and defines what type of research is to be conducted, whether it is exploratory, qualitative, or quantitative in nature. Once the business information needs have been defined, then study design is established.

It is important to adhere always to strict ethical research principles when implementing a study. This is one reason it is generally recommended to use a third party to conduct a market research survey. The business needs can sometimes cloud the objectives at hand and a survey can be designed that leads respondents to specific answers. A professional market researcher should always have the ability to push back if the business need impedes on ethical research design. The Council of American Survey Research Organizations (CASRO) rules outline standards of ethical conduct for the industry. You can access the code of standards at *www.casro.org/codeofstandards.cfm*.

Sound methodology

It is important to understand the research implications of the survey design regardless of whether the survey is for an Internet or a telephone audience. A sound methodology ensures that research principles are adhered to in order to report objective and correct data. For example, sometimes a question can be written in a leading way that drives respondents to give a more favorable rating. The question order can also create a bias effect and impact how subsequent questions are answered.

The length of a survey and the impact on customer survey fatigue must also be taken into account. There are some subtle, but important, factors for online questionnaires that must be understood because unlike a telephone survey, Internet surveys do not have the advantage of having a person to guide a respondent through a survey. These subtle differences affect the data differently. Ensure that the questions can be administered independently of any human guide. Also ensure that the questions can be displayed in a manner that can easily be understood by the respondent. Evaluating the potential affects alongside technology, administration, and business needs will help determine whether a phone or Internet survey should be conducted and will help guide how certain questions are asked.

Technology efficiency

While technology has improved the quality, speed, and efficiency of Internet surveys, there is still much room for improvement in online survey tools. Whenever a specific survey design issue is considered, it is important to know how the technology will react to the solution. The specific solution may not be a wise choice if extra development is required.

It is especially important that the programming rules for a study not be overly complex. Single response, multiple response, scale, open-ended response, or even grid questions are the most common types of questions seen in a survey. Branching rules to skip questions based on respondent qualifications, substituting values into specific questions or answers, or auto-populating variables should all be standard features in a research tool. Auto-rotating a sub-segment of a set of perception questions within a larger auto-rotated group is an example of an overly complex rule. Many tools also have limitations in displaying graphics or referring to files or information outside of a survey. Keep in mind that not every type of rule or question is possible in an Internet survey.

Cost efficiency

Online research studies are almost always inherently cheaper than mail or telephone studies (assuming all other research elements are the same). Nonetheless, it is important to factor in the cost of the research tool, the time saved doing the study in-house versus outsourcing, any extraneous costs such as language translations, or sample acquisition costs.

One important cost element is that some Internet survey tools have built-in processes that are not always the easiest to administer. For example: A survey is being conducted among males and females and every third question is asked of females only. In many technology tools, a specific rule has to be put in place for every third question and not one over-arching rule for every third question. If after a second wave of fielding that rule is changed to every fourth question, then the survey programmer has to rebuild those rules across the entire survey. If the programmer makes a mistake, it could then cause problems in analytics and reporting. This extra time costs money. It is important to consider all cost inputs when building a survey because it can have an effect on the overall outcome of the research project.

Types of studies conducted online

As mentioned in the introduction, a variety of different types of studies can be conducted online. The following is a list of the more common issues using study names typically found in online market research today. The appendix at the end of the book will provide more in-depth descriptions of these types of research.

- Customer satisfaction
- Event- or transactional-based research such as technical support or sales-based surveys
- Relationship-based research measuring the overall health of the relationship with the customer
- Corporate reputation surveys
- Omnibus surveys
- Short and basic surveys conducted with relatively short lead time
- Employee satisfaction surveys
- 360° feedback surveys
- Studies used to evaluate managers generally with a superior, a reporting employee, and an equal colleague
- Employee exit surveys
- Segmentation studies
- Studies which profile a specific target market
- Tracker studies
- Measuring market behaviors and attitudes of a specific audience over a period of time (generally conducted monthly or quarterly)
- Discrete choice/conjoint
- Advertising effectiveness and evaluation research
- Brand evaluation and effectiveness research
- Product research (including Monadic testing and Paired Comparison tests)
- Product testing
- Online message boards

Chapter 3

Setting Up Your Online Survey

Using the criteria outlined in Chapter 2 and assuming that the business professional or researcher has already determined that he or she will conduct a market research survey online, the following set of guidelines will be useful in conducting the survey and analyzing the results. Using these straightforward steps will ensure that the survey is implemented properly and will allow for accurate analysis of the survey results.

Review the objectives of your study

The objectives can have a critical impact on the processes, tools, analytics, and type of researchers involved in the study. A good researcher should be able to take a set of objectives and determine the optimal method to execute the research project. After the objectives have been clearly outlined, the evaluation methodology covered in Chapter 1 should be used to determine if the online survey methodology is appropriate. After this has been confirmed, the same evaluation process can be used to determine the following:

- Who will conduct the survey?
- What tool will be used?
- What types of analytics are required?
- What is the desired reporting outcome?

Each of these questions should be reviewed and assessed prior to launching a survey. Understanding this information before the project is launched can save a researcher thousands of dollars in fielding, processing, or ad hoc requests after the survey has been launched.

Determine who will conduct your survey (for non-researchers)

One of the first questions a non-researcher must ask is, "Should I conduct the survey myself or hire a market research company?" Many online survey tools are available for non-professional researchers to quickly learn and deploy their own survey. SurveyMonkey, Question-Pro, SurveyGizmo, and Qualtrics are all good examples of top online survey tools that allow anyone to conduct an Internet survey.

Tools like QuestionPro and Zoomerang provide Software as a Service (SaaS), meaning that the responses are collected at the third-party's web hosting facility. These tools are generally a little less complex and not feature-rich. Researchers who leverage these tools are required to have a basic knowledge of survey design. In some cases the tools can be quickly learned with a few hours of instruction, generally available on the websites. Tools like Confirmit and Inquisite require researchers to install questionnaire design and server software. The server software needs to be installed at the researcher's facility and generally requires advanced research knowledge to properly leverage it. The difference between the two types of software is analogous to that between Microsoft Excel and Oracle databases.

Market researchers generally advise their clients against conducting a survey on their own because even though anyone can write a question, it does not mean that the question is written properly. Questions should be written in a way that can be easily answered, can meet a specific objective, and do not lead respondents to a specific answer. A good researcher should write questions that are not biased or leading and provide an objective point of view on the findings. At a bare minimum, one approach to reduce costs is to employ a research company to write the questionnaire, and then the fielding and basic data analysis can be performed without the professional market researcher. Even interpretation of the data can be subjective, so it is important to remain objective during review of the data.

Set up the analysis

The analysis that will be conducted as a result of the research study should be determined at the beginning of a study because of the implications on questionnaire design, costs, and types of researchers. For example, a *discrete choice* study must be determined before the survey is established because questions have to be asked in a certain manner. Or, a *customer satisfaction* study must have specific types of questions that allow the researcher to conduct a driver analysis, gap analysis, or simply measure performance based on stated satisfaction. Simply put, determine the type of analysis that will be conducted at the end of the survey so that the study can be properly designed from beginning to end. Failing to do so could increase costs by thousands of dollars.

Determine the survey tool

Not all survey tools are equal. Having a clear idea of the objectives at hand, reporting requirements, and analytic requirements can drive the need for specific types of tools. It is critical that the survey tool evaluation process takes place during the design phase so that the appropriate tool is selected. Chapter 4 thoroughly reviews the processes that should be used to evaluate the appropriate research tool. The Appendix provides an assessment of the various tools available today and contact information for specific vendors.

Design the questionnaire

Designing an online questionnaire is an important part of the online survey process because it affects every succeeding step in the research process. The types of questions, specific branching rules, and layout of the questionnaire will all drive the type of analytics used at the end of the survey and the analytics provide the foundation for making critical business decisions. There are a number of design issues that need to be accounted for and we will cover only the high level strategic issues. We assume that the readers have a decent understanding of the type of research project to be conducted. The strategic issues will be discussed here and the tactical implementation design issues are discussed later on.

Type of questionnaire

When designing an online questionnaire, you must consider the four evaluation trade-offs discussed in Chapter 1: business needs, technology efficiency, costs, and soundness of the methodology. First start with the type of survey that will address the business needs. The following questions will be useful in determining the survey type (e.g., customer satisfaction, product testing, etc):

- What is the business need?
- What is the company trying to measure?
  - Awareness of a product
  - Satisfaction with a company
  - Tracking study measuring overall usage of an assortment of products
  - Buying behaviors
- What is trying to be improved?
  - Satisfaction
  - Awareness
  - Product functionality

- Who is the intended survey audience?
  - Customers
  - Non-customers
- Who is the intended report audience?
  - Marketing professionals
  - Executives
  - Research professionals

Create the foundation of your questionnaire

These questions will guide the researcher in setting up the type of survey to be conducted so that proposals can be written and sent both internally and externally. Once the survey type has been identified, begin designing the survey with the answers to those questions in mind. If the study is for children, ensure that the questions are simple and possibly use more imagery. If the study is for adults, then the questions can be a little more complex, but never make a question overly complex. If customer loyalty is being measured, then conduct a customer satisfaction survey. Keep in mind that in almost any survey, respondents do not read questions with the level of detail that researchers would hope, so keep the questions relatively straightforward.

Use a word-processing document to build your questionnaire

Writing a questionnaire in a word-processing document allows it to be easily edited by multiple parties and allows revisions to be written into the document without having to program anything. Some Internet design tools do allow for the questionnaire to be customized within a tool, but there are generally complications with maintaining edits in the online tool. Sometimes reviewers do not have access to the tool given certain security issues. In many tools, it is difficult to track version control or notate what changes have been made. Given that most reviewers do have access to a word-processing program, it is generally easiest to work with a universal type of document.

Questionnaire flow: Broad to specific

With any type of survey, it is important to consider the flow of the questions. Consider creating an outline to make sure the questions mentioned above are adequately covered and that a proper flow of the survey is maintained. It is generally better to start with broad, high-level questions first and then move into specific questions. This minimizes any type of bias in the survey responses caused by a preceding question. However, sometimes the use of certain types of questions requires survey flow to deviate from this path.

One example is the use of open-ended questions. If asking about general awareness of a service or product using open-ended questions, you may argue that service or product-specific questions should precede overall company-level perception questions. The problem is that answering questions about a specific product may influence perceptions about the overall relationship with the company. Trade-offs sometimes need to be made, but keep in mind the affect on the results when designing the questionnaire flow.

Now, compose a question

Writing an online survey question is no simple task. It is extremely important that ambiguity is removed from questions in online surveys and that questions are written as clearly as possible. Do not use slang, abbreviations, or acronyms that a respondent might not understand. Even if the researcher thinks the acronym is commonly known, it is rarely known by 100 percent of respondents. Images are commonly used in building questions but keep in mind the audience being surveyed. A smiley face might not be appropriate for an educated base of adults aged 40 to 50, but it might be well-suited for children aged 8 to 10.

Should you add color?

Cultures around the world treat colors very differently. While green may have a positive meaning in the U.S., it can have a negative meaning in some Asian countries. Especially in international-based studies, use of colors in an online survey is not advised. Consider using alternative design approaches to demonstrate the intended emphasis or demarcation which would have been made through the application of colors. See Chapter 8: Questionnaire Layout for specific situations where colors have been inappropriately used.

Building specific question types

There are quite a few different types of questions available in Internet surveys to address all kinds of different business issues. Each question type is examined in great detail in the following chapters and covered only briefly here. The chapters will review the primary purpose of the question type, how it addresses specific business issues, the pros and cons of the question type, different implementations, and any other issues specific to the question.

Single-answer question

This question allows only a single answer response. Generally, there is a set of possible answers already provided in the questionnaire.

> What is your gender?
> *(Please select only one)*
> ○ Female
> ○ Male

> Did you stay up past 10:00 last night?
> *(Please select only one)*
> ○ Yes
> ○ No
> ○ Can't remember

Multiple-answer question

This type of question allows a respondent to select more than one answer to a question. A set of answers is provided in the question-naire. Check boxes and a descriptor "Please select all that apply" are generally used for multiple answer questions.

Which of the following activities did you do last year?
(Please select all that apply)
- ○ I ran the Boston Marathon
- ○ I watched more than 20 movies
- ○ I volunteered for the presidential election
- ○ I went on vacation
- ○ I read three books

Grid question

A set of questions and answers can be combined into a grid format to simplify or speed up the question response process.

Which of the following activities did you do last year and plan to do again next year?

(Please select all that apply)

Activity	This year	Next year
I ran the Boston Marathon	○	○
I watched more than 20 movies	○	○
I volunteered for the presidential election	○	○
I went on vacation	○	○
I read three books	○	○

Scale question

A scale question requires that a respondent to answer on a set scale (e.g., a scale of 0 to 10).

Please use a scale from 0 to 10, where a 0 means "not at all important" and a 10 means "extremely important" as you shop for shampoo.

	Not at all Important										Extremely Important
	0	1	2	3	4	5	6	7	8	9	10
Brand	○	○	○	○	○	○	○	○	○	○	○
Price	○	○	○	○	○	○	○	○	○	○	○

Open-ended questions

This is a question with no answer set provided. Respondents are required to "fill in the blank." These questions create difficulties in online surveys because a guide cannot direct the person to answer the question in a specific way. In a telephone survey, a guide may direct respondents to rephrase their answers if they did not understand the question correctly. Additionally, a telephone recruiter can code the answers to open-ended questions as the interview proceeds. These advantages are not available in a web survey. A web survey may add extra work in coding the answers after all surveys have been completed.

Percentage-based question

With percent questions, specific programming must be built into an online questionnaire to ensure that the percents do not exceed certain limits (for example, do not accept anything less than 0 percent or greater than 100 percent). This programming may not be necessary in a phone questionnaire especially if a guide can ensure that the percentages meet specific requirements stated in the questionnaire.

Prioritization question

Questions in which respondents are asked to rank a set of responses.

Graphically-based question

Questions that use images, icons, or video to allow the respondent to make choices, identify issues, or illustrate thoughts.

Establish survey programming rules

In addition to understanding the different types of questions available for an online survey, you must consider the types of programming rules available to enhance a questionnaire. Sometimes you may want a specific population to answer a subset of questions in a study or to skip to another set of questions. Online tools should have the basic functionality to provide this. The following is a list of the types of programming rules that should be included in any basic online survey tool. These programming rules are covered in more detail in Chapter 5.

- **Autofills/Substitution:** Automatically fill in a specific word or phrase into a statement, question, or answer.
- **Branching rules:** Allow respondents to skip or answer a question or set of questions.
- **Order rotation:** Rotates a set of questions or answers randomly or based on a rule.
- **Auto populate:** Automatically populates an answer to a hidden question based on responses to a set of answers.

Field the survey

After the questionnaire has been designed and built into the survey tool, fielding must take place. There are two types of people—customers and non-customers—who are recruited to participate in Internet surveys. For Internet survey tools they are essentially treated the same, but for research purposes they can have an impact on outcomes and decisions. Sometimes they are used in combination when trying to understand a competitor's profile and if they are, ensure that a field is added in the list to distinguish the difference between the two.

Upload the respondent list

One of the key steps required to field the survey is to upload the respondent list into the survey tool. Survey tools require that lists meet specific formats in order for the tool to properly read the list. Most survey tools have a required set of fields that need to be included in the respondent list. Of course, one necessity for an Internet survey is the email address. Any other field is essentially optional or could be based on the survey need. Survey tools generally let you upload a number of other optional fields that allow you to segment responses to questions and gain a better understanding of how different customers feel about certain issues. These sometimes include region, country, income, gender, name, age, or any other information relevant to the study.

Remove duplicate records (De-dup)

De-duping is a fairly common task for research project managers to perform when cleaning client-provided lists. De-duping is the process of identifying duplicate records in a customer or respondent list and removing the duplicate records so that customers or respondents are not sent multiple survey invitations. Many survey tools have this ability built-in and have an automated process to quickly perform the checks. Generally, the de-duping process searches for duplicates on a primary field and for Internet surveys it is usually the email address. Once identified, the tool will reveal the duplicates and request that one of the records be removed or changed. The research tools are especially helpful for maintaining lists over the long term because they can easily add new records and de-dupe them along with the older records already provided.

Using a spreadsheet application for de-duping

If a tool is not available to perform this task, any spreadsheet application will work. However, it can be a bit more difficult to process the records with a spreadsheet application than an automated tool. If using Microsoft Excel, the best method to de-dupe a list is to:

1. Sort by email address
2. Highlight the cells to be de-duped
3. Go to Data > Filter > Advanced Filter
4. Click the box "Unique records only"
5. Press "OK"

Within minutes, the list is quickly and accurately de-duped.

Sampling plan

Building a sound sampling plan is an essential part of the online survey process. A good sampling plan prevents fatigue among respondents and minimizes any costs associated with acquiring the sample. When building a sampling plan, consider two guiding principles that ultimately drive costs: First, the difficulty of acquiring the potential respondent list and second, completion rates (i.e., the number of people that complete the survey divided by the total number that received it, as a percent). Both of these elements affect costs. The harder it is to acquire records for a particular profile, the higher the cost. Completion rates have an inverse relationship to costs—the lower the completion rate, the higher the costs.

Acquire potential respondents

Understanding the difficulty of acquiring the potential respondent list is one step in the process that can be dealt with easily. If it is a customer list, then the only hurdles may be a company's legal or marketing department. If acquiring a non-customer list, a few calls to panel providers will quickly identify how easy or difficult it will be to recruit these respondents.

Response rate versus completion rate

Response rate is the percent of respondents that respond to the survey invitation by clicking on the link in the email or by coming to the introductory page of the survey website. Completion rate is the percent of respondents that complete the survey. Completion does not necessarily mean the entire survey is completed. If a predetermined number of questions is identified for having completed a survey and a respondent hits that threshold, you may call the survey complete.

Response rates and completion rates can vary widely from those of phone and Internet surveys. Many factors can influence response rates and completion rates including subject matter, type of respondents, and the date when they were contacted. For example, respondents contacted on the telephone may be given higher incentives for each completed survey. These recruiters do their best to sell a potential respondent on completing a survey. On the Internet, there is no such persuasion tactic available.

Researchers frequently use the terms "response" and "completion" interchangeably, but they do in fact have separate meanings. A high response rate followed by a low completion rate can point to important problems with the survey. Perhaps there is a programming issue. Maybe the survey is too long, or maybe the wrong respondents were recruited for the type of survey being conducted.

When determining sampling plans, it is probably better to use completion rates rather than response rates. If you need to obtain a specific sample size, then naturally a completion rate must be used.

Bouncebacks

In most client-provided lists, it is common to receive bouncebacks from survey invitations. The impact of having a poor customer list can be detrimental to a research project especially if a sampling plan initially set different assumptions on the number of bouncebacks than were originally estimated. It is common to have a 30 percent or higher bounce rate on the total customer contact list.

Most of the time poor lists are generated because companies do not do not maintain accurate customer contact data. The lists are either incomplete, input incorrectly, not frequently updated, or no central source for maintaining customer contacts exists. In many situations account executives may maintain their own customer lists that are not shared with the larger organization. Customer relationship management tools like Seibel or Salesforce.com are useful tools for companies to centralize their customer contact information and ultimately extract for survey research purposes. Bouncebacks are inevitable in Internet research, but they can be minimized if researchers maintain solid customer lists and work with their IT departments to deal with SPAM.

Calculating response rates with bouncebacks

Researchers often disagree on whether bouncebacks should be included or excluded from calculating response rates for Internet surveys. Some researchers say that the response rate should be a percent of the total customer contact list because that is a reflection of how well a company can reach its customers and the bouncebacks should be included in the denominator of the calculation. The other side contends that if customers never receive the invitation, they do not have an equal chance to respond to the survey. In this situation, the bouncebacks are removed from the response rate calculation.

The decision to include or exclude bouncebacks from the response rate calculation is up to the primary contact conducting the research. Both are legitimate points, but the authors of this book prefer that bouncebacks are removed from the response rate calculation because they do not have an equal chance to respond to the survey.

Completion rates

Completion rates are a bit of an unknown before a survey is fielded. They can be estimated, but not precisely calculated. Completion rates can vary widely depending on the type of survey that is being conducted and the incentive that is provided. Depending on the difficulty of recruiting the respondents and the incentives, completion rates can vary from 0.10 percent to as high as 80 percent. It is difficult to provide a benchmark for completion rates because they vary quite widely.

Surveys that use a third-party list to recruit respondents generally have lower response rates than a list provided by a business to survey its own customers. Also, respondents that fit into a specific niche or

have highly defined survey qualification criteria generally cause completion rates to decrease. Business professionals are usually harder to
recruit than consumers, and within businesses, executives in medium
and large organizations are the most difficult to recruit.

Common incentives

Incentives are commonly used with difficult-to-recruit respondents.
If estimated completion rates are high and obtaining an adequate
sample size is not a problem, then you can generally forgo the use of
incentives. In Internet surveys they are especially helpful for attract-
ing difficult-to-find respondents. If incentives are to be used, establish
an incentive that will have an impact on improving response rates.
Entry into a drawing or providing $5 to each respondent may only
negligibly affect response rates. Obviously, increasing the incentive or
likelihood to win a drawing will increase the chances that someone
completes a survey.

One difficulty with identifying incentives in emails is that they
can increase the chance that the invitation gets caught in SPAM
filters. As noted in the section on SPAM filters (Chapter 5), the use
of phrases that revolve around money typically block an email from
reaching its final destination. Sometimes it is best to minimize the
use of specific words or phrases that get caught in SPAM filters and
provide more detailed information about the incentive on the first
page of the survey. It is important to create a clever message that
indicates that an incentive is being used, but never do so at the
risk of tricking a respondent. This can quickly get an organization
blacklisted or ruin its reputation.

Close the survey

Determining when to close a survey can depend on a number of
factors, including:

- Pressure to deliver final results by a specified time

- Achieving established quotas
- Exhausting available respondents list
- Recruiting expenses outweigh the benefits of adding additional completed surveys
- When an appropriate number of reminders have been sent
- Capturing data within a specified time period

It is generally best to establish a set of priorities during the set-up process for determining when to close the survey. In customer-satisfaction studies, using a company-supplied list (or non-third party list), you will close the survey either when the list of available targets has been exhausted or an acceptable number of completed surveys has been reached. If the potential respondent list is fairly large, then you should prioritize based on achieving an established quota.

In most situations you have to evaluate the trade-offs of different fielding scenarios and the impact on the business from the point of view of cost, business need, and meaningful data. If at all possible, it is best to determine the criteria before fielding starts. This will help keep costs in line with available budgets. However, there are certain situations that require you to evaluate the process while in the field. Sometimes the fielding period may need to be extended or fielding funds may have run out. Whatever the situation is, prepare to be flexible and clever in the decision-making process. Here is a hypothetical example that may help you understand this issue:

Let's call the company Extreme Health Tips. It has an online site dedicated to keeping individuals healthy and decides to conduct an online survey evaluating the market for online health sites. It has a general sense of who its top five competitors are, but isn't positive. It has $15,000 available for fielding the survey, but needs fielding completed within a month. To go about this, Extreme Health Tips will use a third-party supplier to email survey invitations. It has established quotas for its top five competitors (100 each) and added an additional 200 to the quota target for the unknown competitors. Its total survey complete target is 700.

Setting the priorities in this example

Regarding only the logistics and ignoring the methodological implications for now, there are only three things this company needs
to worry about: completing on time, hitting its quotas, and costs.
Since the third-party provider is sending out the survey invitations,
Extreme Health Tips should not have to be overly concerned with
methodology. Evaluating the third-party list provider should have
been completed before the survey was launched and should not affect
the decision on when to close the survey. Extreme Health Tips need
not be concerned about sending reminders as they are not using
their own customer lists.

Before fielding started, Extreme Health Tips prioritized the following:

1. Must complete within one month

2. Not to exceed $15,000 in fielding costs

3. Achieve 100 quota targets for top five competitors

In this case, Extreme Health Tips has a cap on costs and timing,
so these two points should probably be prioritized over quotas (never
overlook the business need behind the quotas though). Quota targets
of 100 may provide slightly more than enough sample to be confident
in the response data. Generally a third-party list provider will either
charge by the number of completed surveys or best-effort attempts.
Either approach is reasonable, but contracting on a survey-complete
base usually comes with a set of guarantees prior to launching the
survey. This makes decision making easier.

Assuming Extreme Health Tips used a best-effort approach, con-
tracted the third-party provider for $10,000, and has an additional
two weeks of fielding available, then it should evaluate the extra
benefits of adding the additional completed surveys during the
second to last week for $2,500. Since it made sense for Extreme
Health Tips to acquire this additional sample because the funding
was available and timing was acceptable, fielding was extended. At
the end of this week, with one more week available, Extreme Health

Tips determined that spending an additional $2,500 was not worth the value of acquiring the additional sample. Quota targets were at 90 percent and the extra time allowed executives to make timely decisions. Even though its quota targets were not achieved, timing and costs improved. Sometimes a situation requires a company to re-evaluate the situation.

Conduct the analysis

After the survey is closed and the data has been cleaned, the analytical process can begin. The analytical process can be as simple as running cross-tabulations or frequencies or as difficult as running a multi-variate regression analysis. As mentioned before, the type of analytics should be determined at the beginning of the study so that the questionnaire can be properly designed to conduct the analysis. At this stage of the process, the data should be set up in a manner that allows the researcher to properly conduct the analysis.

In many cases, the analytical process will take place in specific software tool sets. The online survey tools available today generally only provide the most basic types of analysis like cross-tabulations or significance testing. More complex types of analytics generally use advanced statistical packages like SAS or SPSS. These can include regression, segmentation, or any other type of advanced analytics that generally require advanced tools and researchers to complete.

Report the data

The first step in reporting is to determine how you will report the analysis that is derived from the study. There are many different approaches to building a report and all can be equally valuable. Here are just a few:

- Provide reporting via the survey tool using web links to access the data

- Create scorecards or tables within Microsoft Excel
- Use Microsoft PowerPoint to build reports and presentations
- Use Microsoft Word to build a report

While reporting may seem like a straightforward task, many times clients and vendors spend thousands of extra dollars because reporting expectations were not properly evaluated before the report was put together. Disregarding issues around quality, differing expectations may arise over whether the report should be a "report" versus a "presentation." Reports usually have detailed explanations written in prose that explain data flows, reactions to the data, changes in the data, or notable findings in the data. A presentation has summarized bullets that are highlighted in a spoken presentation. A good presenter will speak to the bullet points, graphs, or pictures on a slide as opposed to reading text from a slide.

Before the reporting process begins it is important to consult with the reporting team on the type of output that is required. Ask the following questions:

1. Is a report needed?
2. Is a presentation needed?
3. Are both needed?

Reporting style can also impact any follow-up or changes needed after the report is completed. Work with the appropriate internal and external clients to determine how the analytical messages should be conveyed. Some people prefer short bullets while others prefer detailed explanations. Some people prefer graphs versus tables or explanations. It is strongly advised that you build an outline before the reporting process begins so that expectations can be clearly defined.

Chapter 4

Selecting a Survey Tool

Numerous survey tools are available on the market today, each providing slightly different functionality, but all serving the same purpose: Internet surveying. It can be a difficult task selecting a survey tool because there are so many to choose from, but if a few guiding principles are followed, the decision can be less cumbersome.

The first step is to determine if the survey will be conducted on a third-party site or if a server will be required to host and conduct the survey. This step will cut the evaluation process in half. If you are doing a simple customer satisfaction survey and not outsourcing to a market research firm, then vendor-hosted software will work adequately. If you are conducting a long-term study that is fielded on a weekly basis then it might make more sense to license the server software so that all of the processing can be maintained in-house. This provides the company a greater sense of respondent privacy and flexibility in building backups for the system.

Web-hosted versus server-based

Online survey tools are offered either as a web-hosted application or a download to a server. With web-hosted, the survey runs on servers owned by the research company. The survey sits on the research company's server and respondents are given a link to go to the site and complete the questionnaire as part of the invitation process. In addition, the data collected resides on the third-party website. The benefit of this type of solution is that you do not need to worry about storage space and site management. Research vendors that offer this type of solution are already set up to have enough storage capacity to run your study as well as many others, and will manage the site to ensure it is always up. The data processing is taken care of, so you receive a clean data set in whatever form you've pre-determined, typically a data file or tabulations.

Server-based tools are downloaded and stored on your company's servers. Respondents are invited to the site you set up to answer the survey and all data is stored on your server. You have complete control of the end-to-end process. This is usually a less expensive option, but it does require more work on your part and you need to know what you're doing. You will need to ensure you have enough server capacity to run the survey and hold the data you're collecting. You'll also need to monitor the survey to ensure it's always up so respondents can get in and complete the questionnaire. In addition, you'll need to perform the data cleaning yourself.

Methodology

Given that the research objective has already been reviewed, the second step is to determine if the survey tool supports the specific type of research *methodology* being conducted. Each website that provides survey tools has a fairly thorough description and list of the types of research its tools support. If the website does not provide a thorough list of the research it supports, do not trust the survey tool and continue your search.

One important element to consider when evaluating online survey tools is to know if the survey tool can be converted to a phone survey. It may not be a requirement, but with just a few instructions for the telephone recruiter, the survey should be conducted just as easily over the phone as it is on the web. If a market research company has a proprietary Internet survey tool, it typically has pre-arranged agreements with telephone recruitment houses to use its technology. In many cases a telephone recruitment company unfamiliar with a specific tool will not conduct the survey.

Technical considerations

Online survey companies offer many of the standard survey features, but also have many unique features. Evaluating the specific features required in a study is prudent. The following outlines many of the features and requirements for online survey platforms.

Survey Types

The type of survey you plan to conduct is an important consideration when selecting a research supplier. Not all online survey tools are set up to support all types of studies. Studies that require complicated multivariate analysis such as conjoint or discrete choice analysis and qualitative projects such as online focus groups or message boards are less common offerings.

Questionnaire design with templates

Many survey tools offer a menu of templates to help you develop a questionnaire for specific types of surveys, while others allow you to create your own templates. Questionnaire templates are general surveys designed for common business issues such as customer satisfaction, employee satisfaction, and brand use, just to name a few. These surveys have standard questions already written and set up in a logical flow. All that needs to be done is customize the questions for your business needs. Additional questions can be added and the questions can be reordered. The obvious benefit of questionnaire templates is that you get a running start on creating a survey. This is especially valuable for survey newbies, but it's also a nice feature for research professionals.

Most companies allow you to select the type of format you want to use, be it radio buttons, drop-down menus, grid questions, or text questions for open-ended responses.

Single-response question

The ability to ask single-response questions is a basic functionality of survey tools and means you are able to ask a question that allows only one answer such as a yes, no, or don't know. This functionality is often used in grid questions where a list of elements, such as brands, is given down the vertical axis and respondents are asked whether they've heard of the brand or not. Only one answer is allowed for each item in the list as in the example below.

Have you ever heard of the following brands of toothpaste?	Yes	No	Don't Know
Brand A	☐	☒	☐
Brand B	☒	☐	☐
Brand C	☐	☐	☒

Multiple-response question

Multiple-response questions allow respondents to select more than one answer. "Please check all that apply" is a typical direction. These types of questions are frequently used when respondents use multiple brands or products, as the example below demonstrates. The response allows brand/product managers to see what their competitive set looks like.

Please indicate which of the following brands you have used in the past 3 months. Please check all that apply.

	Used Past Week	Used Past Month	Used Past 3 Months	Used Past Year	Never Used
Brand A	☒	☒	☒	☐	☐
Brand B	☐	☐	☒	☒	☐
Brand C	☐	☐	☐	☐	☒

Scale question

The ability to ask scale questions is a typical feature of online survey tools. A scale question may also be called a rating question or a matrix question. Not all survey tools allow scale flexibility—the ability to accommodate 5-, 7-, or 10-point scales. Be sure the survey tool can accommodate the number of scale points and end points you want to use.

Below is a list of features that can be found on a computer. For each of the product features, please indicate how likely you would be to use that feature.

	1 = Not at all likely	2 = Somewhat unlikely	3 = Neither likely nor unlikely	4 = Somewhat likely	5 = Very likely
Copy CDs to the HD	☐	☐	☐	☐	☐
Listen to music	☐	☐	☐	☐	☐
Watch movies on DVD	☐	☐	☐	☐	☐
Download music	☐	☐	☐	☐	☐

Matrix question with double response

This question type requires two answers within one row. It is often used to save time, and allows you to collect a lot of information within a table.

For each brand please indicate if you have ever bought the brand and how likely you are to purchase the brand in the next 12 months.

	Ever Bought Brand		Likelihood to purchase the brand in the next 12 months				
	Yes	No	1 = Not at all likely	2 = Somewhat unlikely	3 = Neither likely nor unlikely	4 = Somewhat likely	5 = Very likely
Brand A	☐	☐	☐	☐	☐	☐	☐
Brand B	☐	☐	☐	☐	☐	☐	☐
Brand C	☐	☐	☐	☐	☐	☐	☐

Open-ended question

All online surveys have the ability to capture open-ended responses by showing a text box for respondents to type in their comments. However, some companies prefer limited open-ended questions such as character-limited text boxes, one-line text boxes, and numeric text boxes. With character-limited text boxes, respondents are permitted a specific number of characters to answer the question. An example of where this type of question might be used is if you ask respondents to provide key words or phrases that come to mind when they think of a product or service.

Similar to limited-text boxes is the one-line, open-ended response question, which gives the respondent only one line for an answer. It is often used for unaided brand recall where the respondent only needs to write in the brand name. Numeric text boxes are used for questions that require the respondent to write in a number to a question such as, "What percentage of your time online is used for professional reasons?" or "How many children do you have in each of the following age ranges?" Most survey tools have the ability to put parameters around numeric text boxes, so that answers should add up to 100 percent.

Graphics capabilities

Most survey tools let you upload graphic images. However, you should investigate the format needed and any restrictions on file size. There usually are such restrictions and it's important to keep that in mind—it has implications for survey length depending on the types of Internet connection respondents have. Larger images take longer to download and you may run the risk of losing respondents with slower Internet connections who get impatient waiting for the image to download.

Streaming video capabilities

The ability to stream video within the site is much less common for online survey companies. Some companies get around stream-ing video on the site by embedding a URL directing respondents to the video image that resides elsewhere. The biggest issue with this approach is that once off the survey host site, respondents may not come back and finish the survey. You may be able to address this with redirect links that push the respondent back to the survey after the video is complete or by setting the video up to open as a separate window. In any event, if you plan to show video, make sure you fully understand what the survey company is able to do and test how it will work for respondents.

Skip logic

Skip logic allows the respondent to skip questions. You may decide to have respondents skip a question based on prior answers within the survey or to set up a question tree that, for example, allows men to get one set of questions while women get another. The ability to impose skip logic in the questionnaire can save you time on a survey and keep the respondent from getting annoyed with redundant or inappropriate questions.

Auto-fill or piping

Auto-filling, pre-populating, or piping refers to the capability of the survey tool to pull information gathered earlier in the survey and insert it into a later question. For example, if a respondent says she uses Brand A toothpaste most often, subsequent questions about the brand used most often can have the name "Brand A" automati-cally inserted. The most notable benefit of this feature is the clarity it provides. If the respondent says his favorite soda brand is Dr. Pepper, piping that answer in later in the survey ensures that the respondent and researcher are on the same page when talking about favorite brand. Not all online survey tools have this capability so if it's important to you, make sure it's offered.

Required questions

Required questions are settings you impose on a question that prevent a respondent from advancing further through the survey until he gives an answer.

Error messages

Some survey tools offer as a feature an error message that pops up when a respondent attempts to answer incorrectly, such as trying to input multiple answers when the directions ask for only one.

Help link

Some survey tools allow you to include a help link at the bottom of each survey page for respondents to use if they have a question on how to interpret a question, or have some kind of problem with the survey. This is a great feature, but not a common one and it may cost more to include since it requires someone available real time to answer questions.

Pause or bookmark

A pause feature, also sometimes called the bookmark feature, allows respondents to stop the survey at any point and come back to it later, picking up at the point they left off. This is a convenient feature for respondents and may well help increase response rates, particularly with long surveys.

Back button

A back button allows respondents to go back within the survey to change their answers. There is some debate in research circles as to whether it is a good idea to let respondents change answers. Some fear respondents will recognize changing an answer could shorten the survey length and will go back to do just that. Not all survey companies offer this feature.

Survey integration

A few online survey companies can handle mixed methodologies—data gathered online as well as over the phone, in the mail, or via kiosks. This is obviously a big advantage if you're running a study with mixed methods, but it is a service not a commonly offered.

Visual customization

The degree to which survey tools can customize the look of the survey varies greatly. Most survey tools allow you to upload your company logo, but some tools only allow you to show the logo on a welcome page while other tools can include your logo on each page. The ability to modify fonts and colors is also a feature that most online survey companies can accommodate. Fewer are able to customize the survey to such an extent that it looks like it's coming from your company.

Contact record management

More and more companies are trying to integrate customer data from several places to provide a holistic picture of the client. Several survey tools allow you to pull in records from CRM systems as part of the sample list and similarly amend survey records to the customer data profile. Other companies have tools that allow you to perform basic record management housekeeping such as de-duplicating records, sorting records, and tracking responses.

List management

More online research suppliers are providing tools for list management as part of their offering. With many companies, you can upload, edit, and store your contacts in one place. You can also integrate your contact list with CRM solutions and other internal company contact lists such as suppliers, employees, customers, and partners. This capability enables you to deploy surveys across all touch points of the company for a holistic view of the business.

Survey invitations

There are several ways to send survey invitations. Most online research companies offer the functionality to send survey invites via email to contacts from internal databases, third-party lists, or panel samples. Posting a URL link to the survey on your company's website is another common way to collect responses. Some online research companies also provide the ability to create pop-up invitations on your website that you can program to appear either at random, at specified intervals, to every site visitor, or to new site visitors only.

Tabs

Tabs—or tabulated data—are summarized data usually presented in a spreadsheet format, though sometimes instead provided in a word-processing format. Not all suppliers provide tabs as part of the deliverables. We highly recommend that you always request a set of tabs as part of the deliverables because clients frequently have quick questions that can easily be answered with a well-thought-out set of tabs. It is also important to ask about the tab format. In our experience, a spreadsheet format is much easier to use than a word-processing format.

Tabs should come with a table of contents, but you may need to ask to make sure summary statistics such as mean and standard deviation are included. Including summaries such as top or bottom box ratings (e.g., a summary of the percentage of 8, 9, and 10 scores or 1, 2, and 3 ratings when using a 10-point scale) can be helpful and save a lot of time. You should specify at the start of the project how top box or bottom box rating will be summarized. In addition, tables that summarize data across a variety of attributes can be helpful for analysis.

Here's an example of a summary table of the top percentage ratings for brand attributes.

Brand Attributes: *% of respondents who rated as 8, 9, or 10 on a 10-point scale*

	Total Sample	Men	Women
Convenient	32	46	28
Uses the freshest ingredients	26	25	28
Easy to open packaging	41	40	42
Comes in the flavors I want	36	22	44

Filters

A filter is another way to dissect the data and usually involves applying another criterion to responses. Using the example above, you could apply an age filter on top of the gender crosstab to assess whether women of different ages give different ratings.

Below is an example of an age filter applied to a summary table of the top percentage ratings for brand attributes. Here we see men give the brand higher ratings than women, and older respondents (40+) in general rate the brand higher.

Brand Attributes: *% of respondents who rated as 8, 9, or 10 on a 10-point scale*

	Total Sample			Men			Women		
Age filter	18-24	25-40	40+	18-24	25-40	40+	18-24	25-40	40+
Convenient	31	35	47	35	40	52	15	25	35

Scorecard results view

Scorecards provide a summarized table of the survey results and can be useful to sales and marketing departments to measure progress on initiatives. Scorecard views should be created and agreed to once the questionnaire is set. Research companies have various ways of creating scorecards with some companies relying on a completely automated process while others manually input the data. Obviously, the amount of human interaction can affect both cost and accuracy. Be sure you ask how scorecards are created. It may also be helpful to look at the scorecard with partial data once the study is launched to make sure data are loading into the appropriate cells and that the metrics included meet business needs. How the scorecard looks and is checked should be part of the initial conversations with the research supplier prior to the study launch.

Analytical toolsets

When selecting a survey tool it is important to think about how you want to analyze the data when the survey is done. All survey companies offer the ability to download the data into some type of format, but it's important to make sure the formats are ones you can use. Typical formats include Microsoft Excel and Access, SPSS, .csv, PDF, and SQL. Excel, Access, SPSS, and SQL allow you to manipulate the data in a variety of ways, while .csv and PDF files are stagnant, meaning you can't manipulate them further, but they do make a nice presentation of the data.

Many survey companies let you download respondent-level data. This can be helpful if you plan to do multivariate analysis or want to trace responses back to the individual, such as showing the verbatim comments for a particular respondent or group of respondents.

With virtually all survey tools, you have the ability to monitor the data in real time and download the data at any point. Data are often shown as bar charts. If possible, take advantage of free trials and make sure to try out the cross-tab and filter functions—these are sometimes clunky and not easy to use. In our experience, any issues with the survey tool cross-tab and filter functions can be managed easily by making sure the data can be downloaded into an analytic program with which you are comfortable, such as Excel. Many research companies also tout the fact that they offer statistical testing. Make sure you fully investigate this functionality if you plan to analyze the data using the survey tool features. We have run across survey tools that have statistical capabilities, but they may not be well documented.

For example, statistical differences might be noted with no reference to the confidence level or statistical test used.

There is an abundance of options available when selecting an online survey tool that you will need to wade through when making your decision. The Appendix provides a summary of the features and functionality currently available from companies. Many companies offer free demonstrations or trial periods to test drive their services. In addition, many companies have tiered packages with increasingly sophisticated features/functionality at different price points so you're sure to find something to meet your budget.

Chapter 5

Common Internet Survey Issues

As we mentioned in Chapter 2, not all surveys should be conducted online. A strict evaluation of the technology limitations, methodological principles, cost requirements, and business needs should be understood to determine whether a survey should be implemented online. There are a number of subtle nuances in using online surveys that should be properly understood because they can ultimately affect results.

The time to complete a survey

Not all surveys are created equal, nor should they be. Each of the four evaluation principles found on page 6 has an impact on survey length. The business need may only require a survey that should be completed in five minutes while a methodological principle may require that a survey last for at least fifteen minutes. Survey length can vary from just a few minutes to up to an hour. Non-researchers have a tendency to add extraneous questions that they think might help justify the business need, but often lead to lengthy surveys and unwarranted survey fatigue. Researchers generally try to push back on survey length and remove as many questions as they can. Regardless of the behaviors of different researchers, leveraging the evaluation principles will help determine an optimum survey length that satisfies the business objectives with high-quality feedback.

There are a number of factors to consider when creating an online survey and determining survey length. They include:

- Total number of questions

- The type of questions (single-answer, multiple-answer, open-ended questions, etc.)

- Respondent target base (demographics)

- Survey attrition

- The complexity of the questions

- The kinds of visual displays

- Incentives

The primary factor that should be used to judge survey length is the amount of time required to complete a survey. The length of time, however, should not govern overall survey length since incentives, survey audience, or other factors could justify a survey that takes a long time to complete. Consider all the factors at play and make a holistic evaluation of the nuances that affect high-quality feedback.

Number of questions in an online survey

The number of questions in a survey and the length of time to complete a survey do not necessarily equate. While a survey with over 300 yes/no questions obviously will take quite a while to complete, 25 yes/no questions will be completed much quicker than 25 thought-provoking multiple answer questions. It is generally advised that on surveys with many questions, incentives should be considered—respondents typically drop out of long surveys before they are complete.

Do not use the mere number of questions to conclude that "a survey is too long" or "we can add more questions."

Type of questions in a survey

Of the many different types of questions that can be used in a survey, each has a different impact on survey length. **Single-answer questions** offering a yes/no answer set are obviously the quickest types to answer—the fewer the possible selections, the easier it is to consider and answer the question. Depending on the size of the answer set, multiple choice questions generally require respondents to take longer to think about the multiple situations that are applicable to the question. The important concept to remember about the relationship between question type and survey length is that complex questions with multiple answers and scenarios will increase the time it takes to complete a survey. (Please refer to Chapter 3 for more detailed definitions of these question types.)

Respondent target base (demographics)

The demographic target of a survey can have an extreme impact on determining how long a survey should be. You should never expect the CEO of a large company will complete a survey that takes 30 minutes, with or without an incentive. Everyone has different perceptions of the appropriate length of a survey and many times this can be determined by evaluating the respondent target base. Even if incentives are provided, CEOs can easily be distracted from an online survey and turn their attention elsewhere. Before proceeding with an online survey with CEOs, seriously consider alternative modes of communication, such as scheduling an appointment with them to complete the survey.

Survey attrition

Keep in mind that people outside of the organization will be completing the survey and they are not likely to care about all the fine details in the questions of a survey. Despite countless hours of thought to refine and write the perfect survey, respondents generally treat these as a burdensome task. To that end, survey length can have an extreme impact on survey attrition. This can be problematic in analytical models, which require full data sets.

Online survey research is different than personal interviews—respondents cannot be persuaded by an individual asking the questions to complete the survey. If individuals decide to leave a survey before it is completed, it is usually impossible to convince them to return and continue. Survey attrition is a big part of online surveys and is directly associated with the length of time to complete a survey.

The effect of visual displays

Visual displays can be quite descriptive and effective if implemented correctly, but they can also be costly and detrimental to a research study. Simple images or videos like those seen in advertisements can be descriptive and entertaining in themselves. Follow-up questions asking about comprehension, quality of the advertisement, or quality of the images can generally be direct, easy to understand, and fairly quick, but visual displays that require lengthy descriptions are an easy way to increase survey attrition because of the length of time to read the information. Ensure that the visual images used in a survey are self-contained descriptions. If respondents become frustrated with a survey because it feels too long, then it is likely that they will quickly exit.

Maps and flow charts are other visual displays commonly used in surveys. The same concept for the effect on the length of time to complete the survey applies here. Keep the maps and flow charts self-contained without too much need for descriptions.

Dependence on survey type

Survey length is also dependent on the type of research being undertaken. In general, when the respondent is asked to explore new ideas or unknown concepts such as those commonly seen in product testing, studies take a bit longer to complete. In these situations, respondents have to think about the unfamiliar concepts. Naturally, this will take longer than something like an attribute in a customer satisfaction research (such as quality of technical support).

SPAM

SPAM is an ever-increasing concern for market research companies conducting Internet surveys. Unfortunately, it is really difficult to combat junk mail options. If you come up with solutions to circumvent junk mail folders, then it is likely that spammers can do the same. There are a few different approaches to dealing with SPAM, but nothing will completely eliminate the problem, only minimize it.

CAN-SPAM Act of 2003

As of January 1, 2004, the CAN-SPAM Act of 2003 became effective (Controlling the Assault of Non-Solicited Pornography and Marketing Act). The law protects consumers from unwanted and unwarranted emails and gives them the right to ask emailers to stop sending them email. The act is the foundation for how all researchers should conduct Internet surveys. Details of the Act can be found at the following address:

http://www.ftc.gov/bcp/edu/pubs/business/ecommerce/bus61.shtm

The law specifically bans false or misleading header information, prohibits deceptive subject lines, ensures an adequate opt-out method is used, and requires commercial email to be identified as advertisements and include the sender's valid physical email address. This law applies more specifically to businesses sending advertisements for products or services and less so to market researchers. However, the principles still apply to Internet surveys. Ensure that all surveys adhere to these standards so that ethical standards are practiced in the market research industry as a whole.

Disclose the sponsor and sender of the survey

Sending unsolicited email to customers or potential respondents is the quickest way to get blacklisted or to violate the CAN-SPAM Act. If at all possible, do not send emails to customers unless they have agreed to receive emails from the host company or a third-party provider. Provide an explicit opt-in opportunity and provide the ability for customers or respondents to easily opt-out of receiving future emails. Repeated offenses can be detrimental to the email host organization so it is important to maintain and update a high-quality "Do Not Disturb" (DND) list. That is, if someone requests to not receive future emails from the host company (opts-out), ensure that the email address is kept indefinitely and never contacted again for research purposes.

The "From" address

One important strategy to reduce the chance of being caught in SPAM filters is to ensure that the "From" address in the email invitation displays an obvious and legitimate address. Random letters or numbers or strange words in the "From" address can easily trigger a SPAM filter. Use an email address that appears to be coming from a legitimate source and clearly identifies the source as a research vendor. See the section on writing email invitations. Here are a few examples of properly formatted "From" addresses:

customercompany@researchcompany.com

customercompany_technicalsupport@researchcompany.com

Research_for_customercompany@researchcompany.com

Email "spoofing" and why to avoid it

"Spoofing" is when an email message's header information has been tampered with to make the email appear to come from someone else. It is a popular tactic used by spammers and con artists. It is also used in the online research industry, but the practice must be avoided. The federal CAN-SPAM law prohibits spoofing and, in an effort to combat SPAM, major ISPs are now adopting authentication systems that flag spoofed emails.

Common words or phrases that get caught in SPAM filters

There are a variety of techniques that SPAM filters use to flag SPAM, but one of the more common is to identify key words and calculate the number of times the words are used. In most cases keywords are assigned values. The more often those keywords are used, the quicker the sum increases to flag the message as SPAM. Obviously, sexually-related content is an easy way to get flagged, but since most research is not involved in that industry, the terms are omitted. The following is a set of common SPAM words or phrases; avoid them when sending out survey invitations if at all possible. Unfortunately, while there are some phrases that are required in survey invitations, it is important to minimize their use.

Note: All words below have been capitalized. The same caution or avoidance should be assumed whether they are capitalized or not.

Words or phrases to avoid	
100% Satisfied	Increase Traffic
4u	Information You Requested
50% Off!	Loans
Accept Credit Cards	Lose Weight
Additional Income	Million Dollars
All Natural	Multi Level Marketing
Amazing	No Gimmicks
Apply Online	No Hidden Costs
Best Price	No-obligation
Billing Address	Opportunity
Buy Direct	Pre-approved
Call Free	Promise You
Call Now!	Removes
Can't Live Without	Reverses Aging
Cash Bonus	Risk Free
Cents On The Dollar	Satisfaction Guaranteed
Click Here	Save $
Collect	Save Up To

Words or phrases to avoid

Compare	Search Engine Listings
Credit	Search Engines
Discount!	See For Yourself
Do It Today	Serious Cash
Double Your Income	Sex
Earn $	Special Promotion
Eliminate Debt	Stop
For Free	Subscribe
Free Leads	Urgent
Free Website	Viagra
Free!	Win
Full Refund	Winner
Giving Away	Work At Home
Hidden	You're A Winner!
Increase sales	

Words or phrases to use with caution

#1	Meet Singles
:Remove	Message Contains
100% Free	Message Has Reached You In Error
100% Guarantee	Message Is Being Sent In Full Compliance
1-800	Message Is Sent In Compliance
1-888	Money
Act Now!	Money Back Guarantee
Affordable	Money On The Internet
All New	Month Trial Offer
Apply Now	Name Brand
As Seen On TV	Never
As Seen On...	No Cost, No Fees
Avoid Bankruptcy	No Obligation
Bargain	Now
Be Considered Spam	Offer
Be Your Own Boss	One Time
Below Is The Result Of Your Feedback Form	One Time Mailing
Buy Recommendation	One Time Message
Call	Online Marketing
Call Toll Free	Online Pharmacy
Cards Accepted	Online Promotion
Cash	Order
Cash In On	Order Now

Words or phrases to use with caution

Casino	Order Today/ Order Status
Check	Orders Shipped By Priority Mail
Claims	Performance
Click / Click Here / Click Below	Phone
Click Here For Removal	Please Read
Click Here To Be Removed	Please Respond With Remove
Click Here To Remove	Potential Earnings
Click To Remove	Price
Collect Your $	Print Out And Fax
Compare Rates	Profits
Confidentiality Assured	Reached You In Error
Congratulations	Real Thing
Consolidate Your Debt	Receive This Message In The Future
Contains $$$	Received This Email Because
Contains Word "Ad"	Received This Email By Mistake
Cost / No Cost	Received This In Error
Credit Card #	Received This Message In Error
Custom Quote	Receiving This Email Because
Dear Fellow Entrepreneur	Receiving This Message Because
Dear Friend	Receiving This Special Message
Dear Homeowner	Receiving This Special Offer
Debt Free	Reduce Body Fat
Deleted From Further Communication	Removal Information
Don't Delete	Removal Instructions
Earn Extra Cash	Remove
Earn Extra Income	Remove As The Subject
Easy Terms	Remove In Subject
Email Marketing	Remove In The Subject
Excluded From Our Mailing	Remove Me In The Subject
Explode Your Business	Remove On The Subject Line
Extra Income	Remove Request
Free	Remove You From Our Mail
F R E E	Remove@
Fast Cash	Removed From Any Further Mail
Featured On TV	Removed From Future Offer
Financial Freedom	Removed From Our In-House Mailing
Financially Independent	Removed From Our List
For Permanent Remove	Removed From Our Mailing
Form	Removed From This Mailing
Free Consultation	Respond With The Word Remove
Free Cruise	Sales

Words or phrases to use with caution

Free Gift	Save $
Free Info	Solution
Free Installation	Special Offer Message
Free Membership	Subject Line Of Remove
Free Offer	Success
Free Preview	The Following Form
Free Yourself	This Is Not A Spam
Further Transmission	This Is Not Spam
Future Mailing	This Message Is Not Spam
Future Promotion	This Message Is Sent In Compliance
Get It Now	Time Limited
Get Out Of Debt	To Be Deleted From Our Database
Get Paid	To Be Removed Click
Get Your Free Sample	To Be Removed Email
Give It Away, Giving It Away	To Be Removed From Future Mail
Great Internet Services	To Be Removed From Our Database
Great Offer	To Be Removed From Our Email List
Guarantee	To Be Removed Go To
Hair Loss Product	To Be Removed Mailto
Here	To Be Removed Please Click
Home Based	To Be Removed Reply To This Message
Home Business Opportunity	To Be Removed Send An Email
Home Shopping	To Be Removed Send Email
Homebased Business	To Be Removed Send Mail
Income From Home	To Be Taken Off
Increase Sales	To Remove From Mailing
Increase Your Revenue	Unsecured Debt Or Credit
Increase Your Sales	Unsolicited
Incredible Deal	Unsubscribe
Info You Requested	Us Dollars
Insurance	Vacation
Internet Market	Visit Our Web Site
Investment / No Investment	Visit Our Website
Investment Decision	Web Traffic
Join Millions	Webmasters Only
Joke Of The Day	Weight Loss
Legal	While Supplies Last
Life Insurance Quote	Why Pay More?
Limited Time Offer	Wife
Lose	With The Subject Remove
Lose Inches	Work From Home

Words or phrases to use with caution	
Mailto:Remove	You Have Won
Mailto:Unsub	You Wish To Be Removed
Make $	Your Business On The Internet
Making Money Online	Your Email Removed
Marketing	Your Time And Interest
Marketing Solutions	You've Been Selected

ISPs and blacklists

Customers' companies are not the only ones who have blacklists. Internet Service Providers (ISPs) also have blacklists and it is especially important for market research companies to ensure they are not on these lists. These blacklists are technically referred to as Domain Name Service (DNS) Blacklists. Independent consortiums usually provide ISPs with these lists. Universities and larger organizations are most likely to subscribe to these lists. Information technology employees are typically responsible for checking against these lists and working with the consortiums to ensure they are not on the lists. The following are a few of the more commonly used online sources to verify if a company is blacklisted:

www.spamhaus.org

www.spamcop.net

www.mail-abuse.com

www.njabl.org

Each of these sites provides the ability to check if a specific Internet Protocol (IP: a specific address given to each domain name) address is blacklisted. If the company in question is on one of these blacklists, contact the respective site and inform them of the reasons why the specific company should not be blacklisted. A few years ago, these blacklist companies were reluctant to remove people from these lists because spammers were doing everything they could to remove themselves from these lists. However, after a few successful lawsuits from legitimate email providers, the blacklist companies are a little more open to removing companies from their lists.

Dealing with the customer's company

One approach is to ensure that customers can receive emails from the domain address that is sending the email invitation. (A domain address is the part of an email after the "@" symbol; for example, yahoo.com.) Many companies have blacklists that prevent specific email addresses from sending them unsolicited email. Companies today are now purchasing software to specifically combat SPAM such as the SPAM firewall from Barracuda Networks. McAfee and Symantec also offer software firewalls that can be integrated into email systems to prevent SPAM. It is important to actively communicate with customers to ensure they can receive emails from the host site. Customers can enter a domain address into their SPAM filter so that they can receive email from that specific domain.

Dealing with irate customers or respondents
who have already opted-out

In some situations customers will send an email to the host company saying that they already subscribed to the opt-out list and are upset that they were contacted again for survey purposes. Experience shows that in most cases the customer or respondent provided the host company two different email addresses and only opted-out with one of the email addresses. Ask customers or respondents if they have more than one email address and ensure them that all of their email addresses will be removed from future mailings. If the host company is at fault, then apologize profusely.

Mixed mode methodology

Mixing telephone and web responses is a fairly common practice because it can minimize costs among difficult-to-recruit respondents. There are a few different situations when a mixed mode methodology is used and in some situations researchers abandon one methodology in favor of another. One of the more common implementations is to start with a web survey and then switch to a phone survey if sample sizes are not large enough. Another variation is when a company wants to communicate with a wide variety of customers, from administrative staff to executives. Executives are typically hard to connect with for online surveys because an executive assistant often screens their email. In many cases, a personal telephone call is the only method to get in touch with them. Regardless of the exact approach being used, it is important to recognize that there are subtle differences in the amount and type of responses received using different modes of survey communication.

Advantages and disadvantages

Mixing telephone, web, mail, or interactive voice recordings (IVR) survey responses has its advantages and disadvantages. One of its advantages is that a mixed methodology is helpful in increasing response rates. It has been shown that improvements in response rates are highest when switching between visual- based surveys and aural-based surveys. One of its drawbacks is that respondents tend to answer differently to aural-based surveys than to visual-based surveys. There are also subtle differences in how people react to scale-based questions in a survey. In a study evaluating differences on satisfaction scales, respondents who participated in aural surveys were more likely to answer at the extreme ends of the scale versus those who participated in web surveys.*

The data changes that result from a mixed mode methodology can sometimes be a critical issue especially if a compensation-based metric is used in the survey. It is therefore important to understand the differences so that changes in the data can be properly anticipated and altered if needed.

---

* *The Effects of Mode and Format on Answers to Scalar Questions in Telephone and Web Surveys,* Christian, Dillman, and Smyth, *www.sesrc.wsu.edu/dillman/papers. htm*

Online population: cultural and behavioral factors

One important factor to thoroughly understand is whether the online population is representative of the population being examined as well as the overall market population. Most families and businesses in developed markets did not approach full Internet connection rates until about 2000. If a portion of a population being examined is not connected to the Internet it could wreak havoc on the results. There are still populations that are less connected (such as young children) that should generally be avoided for mixed mode methodologies. There are subtle demographic, behavioral, and attitudinal differences in subsets of populations that could have dramatic effects on the results of a study. If the respondents do not mirror the target audience and the general population then it is possible that quota or weighting techniques should be applied to ensure accuracy between sets of data.

Differences in interviewing environment

Studies have shown differences in how people respond to different interviewing methodologies. In general, similar communication methods produce similar results. For example, results from oral surveys such as telephone and in-person interviews will have similar results and those will be different from visual type surveys such as online and self-administered paper surveys.*

Programming rules

One of the important differences between a web survey and other survey types is that a web survey has the ability to create certain types of programming rules. It can hide certain questions from a

---

* *Response Rate and Measurement Differences in Mixed Mode Surveys Using Mail, Telephone, Interactive Voice Response and the Internet.* Dillman, Phelps, Tortora, Swift, Kohrell, Berck, *www.sesrc.wsu.edu/dillman/papers.htm*

subset of the survey audience or fill in an answer from a previous question into a future question. Phone surveys can provide this level of complexity, but mail and IVR studies generally do not. This dynamic survey ability can make the questions more targeted to a specific audience, which can have an impact on how the entire data set is interpreted by the researcher.

Survey administration

Another unique feature of web surveys is that they are self-administered, whereas a telephone survey has a guide. Web survey respondents can complete the survey at their own pace and time whereas in telephone surveys the respondent is pressured to complete the survey in one attempt and in a timely matter. A guide may create unknown pressures on a respondent and influence how that respondent answers questions. A guide may also influence the level of honesty a respondent provides.

Visual cues

The lack of visual cues in a telephone survey can influence the level of detail of a particular message being examined. As the cliché goes, "a picture is worth a thousand words." The use of images in web surveys can be extremely helpful in evaluating specific products or services. Where an image can quickly describe the details of a product or service it may take valuable minutes to explain the message on the telephone. This difference can have an impact on the type of questions and ultimately the type of results available.

Changing survey modality in successive waves

Changing survey modalities in successive waves of research studies will most likely have an impact on the historical data trends. Similar to mixed mode studies, it is important to understand the impact of using different modalities to conduct your survey research. The same principles apply, but one important technique is recommended: parallel testing. Parallel testing is an exact replication of the survey process generally with one variable in the study changed. It should be used when a study that is repeated over time is switching survey methods. In the case of changing modalities, everything between the two different modes should be exactly the same except that a different modality is used. The same questionnaire, the same population base, and the same research company should all be used to conduct both studies.

Evaluating trade-offs when changing survey modalities

In a perfect scenario, sample sizes should be the same between the two different studies, but sometimes there are constraints that prevent this. This is where the trade-off analysis becomes really important, especially if there are compensation-based metrics being calculated from one of the studies. For example, a business is conducting a telephone technical support satisfaction survey and uses overall satisfaction as a measure of compensation. The company may already have a difficult time meeting quota requirements on a quarterly basis for which the compensation-based metric is calculated. In this case, it is important to maintain a large enough sample size in the telephone survey while the parallel testing is conducted. It is probably best to split the sample 75 percent for the telephone survey and 25 percent for the web survey. Of course it will be important to examine the confidence intervals of the two populations in order to determine an appropriate split. The exact proportion should be a decision left to the researcher in charge.

A reduction in sample size may have an impact on the variability in the data. Confidence intervals will increase and it is possible that the data may fluctuate because the sample is not as representative of the overall population. Ideally, a parallel test should occur that completely mirrors the original process. However, difficulties in achieving sample sizes that are accurate representations of the total customer population require a reduction in sample sizes in order to make a smooth transition to a new modality.

Length of time for conducting a parallel test

Researchers might disagree on exactly how parallel testing should be implemented, but most will agree that at least some level of parallel testing should take place when changing survey modalities. At the very minimum, the parallel testing should occur for at least one survey cycle for most types of studies that are repeated over time—tracking studies, satisfaction studies, advertising and brand studies, or any other studies that are more concerned with trend analysis and less concerned with point-in-time analysis. Once you feel comfortable that the parallel tests were implemented successfully and accurate data has been collected, you can make the judgment to turn off the old survey mode and completely switch to the new mode.

Analyzing data for parallel test

While it is imperative that the implementation methodologies be mirrored for both modes in a parallel test, the analytical techniques should also be applied to both. At a very minimum, straightforward distributions should be compared for all questions in the studies. If there are unique analytical techniques used in the old study, they should be replicated for the new one. The goal is not only to identify differences in the results but also to look for key patterns that show a consistent shift in the data.

For example, imagine a branding study to evaluate the level of familiarity of a number of products for a company. The questions use 0 to 10 scales, which are consistently applied for both modes and all questions. If both studies are mirrored well, and if the overall average for all questions in the phone study is 8.2 while the overall average in the web study is 7.5, then a statistically significant difference is identified between the studies.

Adjusting the data for the parallel test

If the data are statistically the same across both modalities then it might be best to proceed with the modality switch and not make any adjustments. If after a thorough examination of the data inconsistencies still exist, an adjustment to the historical data or future data should be considered. An adjustment (or weighting) to the data can take place at the respondent level or at the aggregated, reported data (or means) level. Experienced professional researchers who are familiar with these types of tests should lead the implementation of the study, conduct it, and most importantly make any necessary adjustments to the data if needed.

The easiest strategy is to adjust historical reported data once, and then measure all trends against this newly adjusted data. The downside is that differences in the current parallel test may not reflect historical data. One difference that cannot be controlled for in this case is the "time" element. Another option is to consider weighting the respondent level data in future waves of the study. Methodologically this is satisfactory, but from an administration perspective this task could become quite cumbersome in the future. Another approach is to leave the data alone and note that the differences could be caused by the changes in methods.

Using parallel tests to switch vendors

The processes outlined above ensure the best possible methodological approach in order to minimize any inconsistencies due to switching modalities. Many of the same principles outlined above also apply when changing vendors. Because different vendors may have slightly different techniques for conducting surveys, a parallel test is recommended to understand if there are differences in the results caused by using a new vendor. The same principles regarding the implementation strategies and analysis also apply here. Unfortunately, not all variables can be controlled, so adjusting the data requires a thorough understanding of the processes for both vendors and an experienced researcher to evaluate the data.

Updating the survey while in the field

Surveys are not always implemented error free and these situations force business owners to consider changing the questionnaire during fielding or potentially re-fielding if needed. After a survey has started and some element of the survey is changed in mid-or post-fielding, the data results of the two variations of the surveys most likely should not be compared. Although unintended, a change to one question in the survey can potentially affect how a respondent answers the rest of the questions throughout the survey. Once again, the trade-offs of administration, technology, methodology, and business needs require a thorough evaluation to determine if a change to the survey should be made after it has already been launched. Naturally, cost is an implication that would factor into the business need.

For example, if one question was asked in error and does not affect branching rules and is not a critical business need, then it is probably best to leave the survey unchanged. If the question incorrectly asked is the primary dependent variable being measured in the planned analysis, then that entire analytical approach is flawed. In this case it might be best to make the survey change and start over fielding.

Survey frequency fatigue

Survey frequency fatigue is a research concern that is encountered regardless of the mode of survey communication. It is, however, a commonly discussed issue with web surveys because the significant costs savings in web surveys allows businesses to conduct surveys more frequently. Additionally, page after page of survey questions may affect respondents differently than a guide on a telephone since there is no encouragement to continue with the survey. Ultimately, sending too many surveys to any one individual can have a negative impact on that customer's experience, but may allow an organization to better monitor and more closely understand its customer base. Too few surveys can lead to an incomplete analysis of a customer base, but will not affect a customer's relationship with a business. The trick is to find the sweet spot.

In order to prevent survey frequency fatigue, researchers implement a "frequency fatigue rule" that prevents respondents from answering a survey from the same company for a set number of days. Frequency fatigue rules are determined based on a number of criteria that must be evaluated to properly determine the rules for the research project being undertaken.

Fatigue and customer lists

Survey frequency fatigue is generally not an issue when a third-party list is used to conduct the survey. It is more important when using a list provided by the company that is conducting or commissioning the survey. If using a third-party list, the third party should be managing the fatigue of panelists through the use of task appropriate incentives. Panel companies monitor the level of incentive required to keep a panelist engaged enough in a survey to complete it. If a customer list is used, survey frequency fatigue should be closely monitored so as to not exhaust the sample for the sake of achieving response quotas.

This can be assessed by reviewing completes by question in real time and assessing the percentage of respondents that drop out at each question.

Setting the frequency fatigue rule

There is no research standard today for setting frequency fatigue rules. Frequency fatigue rules should be set based on the set of trade-offs covered in this book. The following set of criteria should be considered when evaluating the trade-offs to set frequency fatigue rules.

Frequency fatigue and complete versus incomplete surveys

Many researchers believe a different set of frequency fatigue rules should be used for survey respondents and non-respondents. They reason that it is generally not wise to continue with the same sample wave after wave. It is possible that if the same sample is surveyed, it might not be an accurate representation of the overall sample —the sample may be skewed based on an attitudinal attribute or behavioral quality. At the very minimum, frequency fatigue rules for complete surveys should rarely, if ever, be less than fatigue rules for incomplete surveys.

Panel-supplied respondents

Many times panels require their own fatigue rules. Panel managers need to properly balance a constant touch on the panel with overuse of the panel. Panel managers will require different frequency fatigue lengths depending on the costs to recruit and type of sample base being requested.

Frequency fatigue and types of surveys

The type of survey being conducted will have an impact on the frequency fatigue rules. Shorter surveys like an event-based satisfaction survey (e.g., technical support survey with fifteen questions) can have fatigue rules set as short as fifteen days or as long as six months. Surveys with more questions—like product testing or relationship based customer satisfaction surveys—should be set at as little as three months or as high as twelve months. If a survey is long and a customer successfully completed the survey, do not overburden the respondent with additional invitations to more surveys in the near future. The research industry needs respondents and exhausting them will obviously impact the industry.

Incentives affect frequency fatigue

Incentives may allow organizations to decrease the interval between sending out surveys. The more attractive the incentive the better chance you have of shortening the frequency fatigue rule.

Number of days for frequency fatigue rules

This table shows recommended guidelines for establishing frequency fatigue rule by type of survey:

Survey Type	Length of time	Invitations sent: no customer response	Invitations sent: customer response
Customer satisfaction: event-based survey	less than 5 minutes	no less than 45 days	no less than 90 days
Customer satisfaction: relationship-based survey	10-30 minutes	no less than 90 days	no less than 180 days
Omnibus surveys	less than 5 minutes	no less than 30 days	no less than 45 days
Product concept	20 minutes	no less than 90 days	no less than 180 days
Employee satisfaction	10-30 minutes	no less than 90 days	no less than 180 days
Advertising effectiveness	5-30 minutes	no less than 90 days	no less than 180 days

Random sampling error and non-sampling error

There are two types of error in market research surveys, *random sampling error* and *non-sampling error*. Random sampling error accounts for any differences between the sample and the overall population. Statistical calculators are good tools to calculate the affects of random sampling error. Non-sampling error is any type of error in the survey data that cannot be measured by a statistical tool. It exists in almost all surveys, but there is little that can be done to estimate the impact. The goal is to minimize the impact of non-sampling error.

There are unique features of web survey tools that introduce non-sampling errors into a survey design. While there are many types of non-sampling error, only the error attributed to Internet surveys will be reviewed here. Many of the pitfalls of the following topics will be discussed in more detail throughout the book, but a high level overview is provided below.

Survey response error

Survey response error is generally attributed to poor questionnaire design. This is caused either by poor graphic design or poorly written questions or instructions. It is extremely important that surveys be written in a simple and very clear manner. For example, if there are scales questions in a survey, it must be very obvious and clear whether the scale is displayed in a positive to negative or negative to positive direction.

Survey programming error

Survey programming errors are attributed to either programmers who do not properly build an online survey per the instructions provided by the designer of the questionnaire, or to incomplete instructions from the survey designer. You can minimize these problems by adding an additional person to perform quality assurance checks on both the content of the questionnaire and the ability to take the questionnaire online. Testing the survey prior to launch by both the programmers and the survey writer can also ensure the programming is correct.

Data processing error

Data processing errors are generally created once the survey has completed fielding and someone is checking the final data set. Some online research tools allow researchers to review the data within the tool. If the tool has a bug in its software, it may prevent proper coding of open-ended questions or not allow for a thorough review of the data.

Chapter 6

Designing Survey Invitations

Respondents participate in a study because they feel there is a benefit to themselves. The benefit can either be a financial incentive or the idea that their feedback is making the overall situation better for them or the general population. Even though respondents may benefit, always remember that they are doing you a favor. Many respondents are only slightly tuned in to your objectives, so introducing complexities can quickly reduce your chances for recruitment success. Focus on the benefits for the respondent, keep it simple, and be brief. Survey response will be much better if these guidelines are followed.

Crafting a survey invitation is one of the trickiest aspects of an online research study. An email invitation has to be attractive enough to entice the audience to participate, but cannot be so flashy that it looks like an advertisement. The invitation has to clearly identify the party that is sending the invitation in the "From" line and the "Subject" line so that it does not look like it is being spoofed or is caught as SPAM. There are also many research standards implemented by industry-wide research consortiums (like CASRO), which require certain types of invitations to be written in a specific manner depending on the type of study.

In most situations, research organizations should use online panels or a client-provided sample with people that have already consented to receive emails from third-party organizations. Some organizations are even considering requiring that potential respondents provide permission to receive research email invitations before a study is launched. Whether the sponsoring company is revealed or not (also known as a blind study), it is suggested that some sort of description is provided in the invitation outlining the purpose of the email and possibly the study. Most researchers generally agree that it is best to be as open as possible, but sometimes research requirements limit the amount of information revealed in an invitation. Survey invitations have changed rapidly over the last few years. There are two types of online survey invitations used today, HTML-based and text-based invitations.

HTML-based invitations provide the sponsor and hosting research company the ability to make the survey more enticing through the use of graphics or images. Many times these graphics and images are representative of either the sponsoring company or the hosting research company. While there is no documented proof that these types of survey invitations increase or decrease participation rates, they do provide a sense of elegance.

Text-based invitations use only text in an email. The text is the only tool used to describe the study, its intentions, or the company sponsoring or hosting the survey.

Developments in survey invitations

Up until about 2004, most invitations were text-based because many people did not have email systems capable of receiving HTML-based invitations. Now, even if an email system cannot display HTML or the user has HTML turned off, the systems can interpret the information to a certain extent and still display it in an email. Undeveloped countries may still require the use of text emails, but this is quickly changing. If the study is being conducted in a developed country, it is highly unlikely that problems will occur because of an HTML-based invitation.

Online survey invitations have taken on many different forms over the last couple of years including new techniques like flash pop-ups on a web page. Some of these alternative approaches are becoming so common that it is difficult to surf online without being invited to participate in a study. Yahoo.com and ESPN.com are two heavily trafficked websites that use these alternative approaches.

Crafting an email invitation

Crafting an email invitation is a subtle art that requires a bit of experience. Novices may use inflammatory language or bias respondents before they even have seen questions in a study. It is important that the language is carefully considered in a survey invitation and maintains proper objectivity. There is no sense in upsetting a customer or potential customers simply from a survey invitation.

There are a few basic tricks to writing a proper online survey invitation that are universal regardless of the type of research being conducted:

- **Keep the survey invitation simple**

  Many times survey creators feel they are acting in the best interests of respondents by including every piece of information they can think of—the survey objectives, anonymity requirements, timing, logistics, legal information, etc. The list can go on for quite a while and ultimately respondents pay the price. Remember, respondents are doing you a favor; respect their time.

- **Identify the benefit to the respondent**

  Clearly identify what the respondent will gain by completing the survey. A clear benefit to the respondent increases response rates and completion rates. The benefit can be a personal benefit like a gift (money, drawing, gift card, donation, etc.), or altruistic—the respondents' feedback will be used to improve the overall situation for all customers.

- **Explain the purpose of the research effort**

  Respondents will not participate in the study if they do not

know what it is about, especially with the increase and threat of
SPAM. State the objectives of the research effort so that respondents are clear about the study they will participate in.

- **State the length of the study**

  Survey length can quickly make a happy customer upset.
  There is no point in making a customer unhappy over a survey. Respondents should know what they are getting into. Do
  not surprise them with an extremely long survey. Also, do not
  underestimate the time needed to complete the survey.

- **Provide instructions on how to be removed from
  the survey list**

  It is likely that the respondent being interviewed was acquired
  via a third-party marketing list or a company-supplied customer
  list. Regardless, customers should be able to remove themselves
  from the email list.

- **Statement of confidentiality/anonymity**

  The current laws in most countries require a person's contact information to remain anonymous. The information the
  respondents supply should not be used for marketing or sales
  purposes and the confidentiality/anonymity statement should
  state this.

- **Study URL must be provided**

  This is an obvious one; show the URL. The URL can be presented
  entirely or may be provided as an abbreviated link (see examples
  below). Without the URL, the study cannot be completed.

- **Disclose the study's host**

  It is extremely important that respondents are told the name of
  the company that is hosting the survey. Too many scammers are
  trying to make a cheap dollar, so it is vital that the company
  hosting the study reveal itself. Respondents are getting more
  savvy about these scammers so it is unlikely that they will participate in the study if the hosting company is not identified.

- **Determine whether the study will be "blind"**

  While this is not a requirement, it is an important factor to consider. A blind study refers to situations in which the company that is paying for the research is not identified. In many types of advertising, brand, and product studies, identifying the company funding the project could bias the responses. Other situations require that the company funding the project is revealed. This is most common in customer satisfaction research.

Email invitation examples

The following email invitations are various examples that can be leveraged for other studies. Each invitation below covers a different type of research objective. Company names are removed from the invitations because of proprietary reasons. The text underlined represents links to a survey website. There are three types of survey invitations covered below:

- Text-based survey invitations
- HTML-based survey invitations
- Pop-up/overlay-based survey invitations

Text-based survey invitations

Although becoming less prevalent, there are still some individuals who will not accept HTML-based surveys because of the fear of viruses, spyware, or SPAM. Text survey invitations are still commonly used today for online research. The benefit is that a respondent will be able to read every part of the message as all email tools display plain text. The drawback is that these survey invitations do not provide flashy images or other tools to entice a respondent to participate. Additionally, web links must be shown in their entirety. They cannot be abbreviated the way they can in an HTML survey invitation.

Text survey invitations are used for almost all types of research. They can be used for customer satisfaction, branding, messaging, product evaluation, or even online message boards. Additionally, in Office 2007 (and most other email applications), the text font shows up as *Consolas*. It is a basic text font that can be unappealing to the eye. However, it is readable by most handhelds and email applications.

Text-based invitation: customer satisfaction (respondent not identified)

Subject Line: Company X Customer Satisfaction Survey
Dear Customer,

On behalf of XYZ Company, we invite you to complete a Customer Satisfaction Survey regarding the services they provide. Your participation in this survey will help XYZ Company to deliver the highest level of service to valued customers like you.

This survey is being conducted by ABC, an independent research company, on behalf of XYZ Company. Please be assured that your privacy is respected and your contact information or individual responses will not be shared with XYZ Company at any time, and will only be shared with XYZ Company with your consent.

To participate in this survey, please click on or copy and paste the following URL into an Internet browser: http://abc.com/xyzsurvey

The survey should take only 10 to 15 minutes to complete.

Thank you for your participation,
ABC Company
Address

To be removed from this survey list, please reply with "Remove" in the subject line.

Text-based invitation: customer satisfaction example 1 (respondent identified)

The primary difference with a respondent identified invitation and a respondent non-identified survey is that the customer's name is piped into the salutation.

Subject Line: Company X Customer Satisfaction Survey
Dear Jane Doe,

On behalf of XYZ Company, we invite you to complete a Customer Satisfaction Survey regarding the services they provide. Your participation in this survey will help XYZ Company to deliver the highest level of service to valued customers like you.

This survey is being conducted by ABC, an independent research company, on behalf of XYZ Company. Please be assured that your privacy is respected and your contact information or individual responses will not be shared with XYZ Company at any time, and will only be shared with XYZ Company with your consent. To participate in this survey, please click on or copy and paste the following URL into an internet browser: *http://abc.com/xyzsurvey*

The survey should take only 10 to 15 minutes to complete.

Thank you for your participation,
ABC company
Address

To be removed from this survey list, please reply with "Remove" in the subject line.

Text-based invitation: customer satisfaction example 2 (respondent identified)

Subject Line: Company X Customer Satisfaction Survey
Dear John Doe,

Company X remains committed to soliciting feedback from its customers regarding its product, services, and processes. Customer feedback is used to identify weaknesses and opportunities to make additional business investments to further enhance its customers' satisfaction.

You are invited to participate in this year's Company X Customer Satisfaction Survey. The survey will be open until DATE and will take approximately ## minutes to complete.

Please click on the link below to access the survey:
http://www.website.com

If you have any questions about the survey, please reply to this email at *companyx@vendor.com*

Company X thanks you for your time and input.
Sincerely,

Program Director name
Director, Respondent Relations
Research Vendor name

Please be assured that your privacy is respected and your contact information or individual responses will not be shared with Company X at any time, and will only be shared with XYZ Company with your consent. To be removed from this survey list, please reply with "Remove" in the subject line.

Text-based invitation: employee satisfaction

The employee satisfaction survey invitation process presents some unique difficulties. One of the methodological goals of an employee satisfaction survey is to ensure employees that their responses will remain anonymous. If the survey invitations are sent from personnel within the company, employees may feel that their responses will not be kept confidential and anonymous. If the survey invitation is sent from a third party, employees may think that the survey is SPAM or junk mail. It may even get caught in junk mail filters.

If an invitation is sent from personnel within the company, it is best to ensure that it comes from the highest-ranking employee in the organization. This demonstrates the seriousness of the survey and the commitment of management to improving employee satisfaction. Additionally, it is important to stress the confidentiality and anonymity of the survey process.

If the invitations are sent from a third party, they must clearly demonstrate that it is being sponsored by the employee's organization. It is also important to identify the sponsoring executive within the invitation. In many situations, a pre-invitation survey letter can be quite useful in improving response rates. A pre-invitation survey letter is sent by someone within the organization—generally the sponsoring executive or employee—stating that a third party will be sending invitations to participate in the survey. The letter prompts employees to anticipate an email from a third party, and many times to turn off personal junk mail filters. The following is an example of a pre-invitation survey:

Text-based invitation: employee satisfaction pre-invitation email

Dear Company X Employee,

Company X values its employees and is committed to providing mechanisms as ways to improving employee satisfaction at Company X. Company X has enlisted the help of Market Research Company Y, a leading marketing research company, to conduct employee research.

The study will take approximately 10 minutes to complete. If you have not completed the survey within 5 business days, Market Research Company Y will send you a reminder letter to ensure you participate in the study.

The study will be open on DATE and remain open until DATE. You can participate any time during this timeframe.

Please be assured that your responses will be kept confidential. You will be provided with a unique study invitation so other employees and Company X, in general, will not be able to identify you. However, if any of your responses suggest that someone has engaged in improper or illegal behavior, your identity may be reported without your permission, if legally required, or otherwise required by company policy.

Log in instructions will be sent to you by PERSON at *survey@companyx. com* (email address).

If you have any questions regarding this, please feel free to reply to this email or write me at (email address).

Sincerely,

Company X contact

Text-based invitation: employee satisfaction survey invitation email

Dear Employee,

I am excited to announce our first annual employee survey. We are committed to working towards improving our business and must do this through your feedback. There is a strong link between employee commitment and business performance and your feedback is essential to driving our growth.

The success of this survey depends on your participation and feedback. Please be honest and forthcoming with your feedback. Please be assured that your responses will remain confidential and anonymous.

The survey is available at:

www.examplesurvey.com/employeesat

Thank you very much for your time and feedback.

Kind regards,
Name, CEO

Text-based invitation: brand evaluation (blind study)

In this example, the sponsoring company is not identified. In customer satisfaction surveys, this rarely occurs because the sponsoring company provides the customer list. CASRO requires that the customer list owner be identified. In branding studies or product evaluation studies hosted by a third party market research company, the sponsoring company is generally not identified.

Dear Jane Doe,

You are invited to participate in a short survey regarding soda and cola advertisements seen on television. The study will take approximately 10 minutes to complete. If you have not completed the survey within 5 business days, Market Research Company Y will send you a reminder letter. If you are qualified and complete the survey, Market Research Company Y will send you an honorarium of $XX for participating in this research project.

Please be assured that your responses will be kept confidential. Your name will not be shared with anyone and your results will be used in aggregate.

You may access the study at: *www.surveyexample.com.*

If you have any questions regarding this, please feel free to reply to this email or contact address@address.com

Sincerely,

Company X contact

Company X

HMTL-based survey invitations

HTML-based survey invitations allow web-based functionality and messages to be embedded in an invitation. These types of survey invitations allow companies to incorporate branding or other messaging that benefit the company in ways outside of what a traditional research study offers. However, in no way should this branding or messaging persuade respondents to provide biased responses or remove the objectivity of a research study. Generally, this type of messaging or branding is limited to company banners (see example below) or background colors that are reflective of company colors.

Another potential benefit of HTML-based surveys is that they help respondents quickly identify the sponsor of the study. Some respondents may react more positively to visual cues. With the ever-increasing burden of SPAM, helping respondents easily identify the company sponsor can have an impact on overall response rates.

HMTL-based survey: respondent identified (blind study)

Survey invitations can be either company identified or blind, meaning the company sponsoring the survey is not identified. With blind surveys, a third party, typically a market research company, is the entity that sends out the invite, but the end client is not identified. Company identified surveys will typically have higher response rates and complete rates, which can translate into cost savings with less sample required to fill the required completed interviews. That said, many companies do not want to identify the company in the survey for fear it will bias the results or tip off the competition. For example, a company that has recently had bad press may not want to identify the company name in the survey as it could lead to lower scores on various measures within the survey. Similarly, a company that is seeking feedback on a new product that has not yet launched may want to conduct a blind study—a respondent could inadvertently leak the product concept to a competitor. Deciding whether to conduct a company-sponsored or blind study is ultimately up to the individual company and depends on the circumstances of that company. Examples of each type of invitation are included below.

HMTL-based survey: company-identified invite

Dear John Smith,

Company A values your opinion and would like to invite you to participate in a short survey regarding product A. The study will take approximately 10 minutes to complete and you will receive an honorarium of $XX for participating in this research project.

Please be assured that your responses will be kept confidential. Your name will not be shared with anyone and your results will be used in aggregate.

You may access the study at: *www.surveyexample.com.*

If you have any questions regarding this, please feel free to reply to this email or contact *address@address.com.*

Sincerely,

Company A contact
Company A

HMTL-based survey: blind invite

Dear Mary Jones,

You are invited to participate in a short survey to provide your opinions of various makes of cars. The study will take approximately 10 minutes to complete. If you are qualified and complete the survey, Market Research Company X will send you an honorarium of $xx for participating in this research project.

If you have not completed the survey within 5 business days, Market Research Company X will send you a reminder letter.

Please be assured that your responses will be kept confidential. Your name will not be shared with anyone and your results will be used in aggregate.

You may access the study at: *www.surveyexample.com.*

If you have any questions regarding this, please feel free to reply to this email or contact *address@address.com.*

Sincerely,

Market Research Company X Contact
Market Research Company X

Pop-up/overlay-based survey invitations

Pop-up/overlay-based survey invitations are seen on specific websites. They are typically used in customer satisfaction research, web evaluation research, brand research, or product research. They can be used for both qualitative and quantitative research and are generally triggered when surfing to a new web page. Many times companies write applications that randomly trigger when a pop-up invitation surfaces.

There are a few different types of technologies used for pop-up/overlay-based invitations. Traditionally, market research companies started using HTML as the technology for surveying people. Unfortunately, they were not the only ones using this technology. Other companies also began using this to make advertisements pop up. As a result, the market created technologies to suppress pop-up web pages. Now, companies are more commonly using DHTML (Dynamic HTML) overlays. The concept is a bit different than traditional pop-ups in that the new image is technically contained within the original web page. From a technical perspective, it does not look like a separate web page. Therefore, pop-up blockers do not register it as a pop-up and it is able to seamlessly appear on the web page.

Pop-ups or overlays are most commonly used when a person

enters a website. While it can be used when a person exits a website, it is not commonly done because the older pop-up technology must be used, which may get caught in pop-up blockers. Since people generally look at multiple web pages, programming scripts are written to trigger an overlay or pop-up after a random number of pages are clicked on. This can be based on the total number of pages across all users or a randomly assigned number of pages for each individual web surfer. Most market research companies have prebuilt applications that can be plugged into the sponsoring research company websites.

Other types of survey invitations

Web technology can be used for a variety of research. In addition to customer satisfaction, advertising and brand research, and product development studies, invitations can also be used for employee satisfaction, 360° studies, and qualitative-type research such as online message boards. Here are a few sample invitations that may be useful.

360° survey invitation

Dear John Doe,

As someone who works with "Johnny Jeans," you have been identified as someone who is qualified to participate in a 360° review of your colleague. The purpose of this research effort is to gather feedback and perspectives on how to best improve standards, processes, and employees at our organization.

The survey is available at: *www.surveyinvite360.com.*

Your responses will be kept completely confidential and will not be shared with Johnny Jeans. Your name will not be directly associated with any of the survey results.

The survey should take no more than 15 minutes to complete.

Thank you very much for your participation. Should you have any questions, please contact your Human Resources department.

To begin the survey, click: *www.surveyinvite360.com.*

Thank you,
Human Resources Department

General blind study

Subject Line: Participate in a study about the types of bleach you use

Dear Name,

You are invited to participate in a study about the types of bleach you use. For completing the survey, you will receive a gift of $XX for your time and feedback.

Please click on the link below to access the survey:

http://website.com/s.asp?ID="Userid"

If you have any questions about the survey, please reply to this email at *studyfocus@vendor.com.*

Thank you for your time and input.
Sincerely,

Program Director name
Director, Respondent Relations
Research Vendor name

General sponsor-revealed study

Subject Line: Participate in a study about the types of bleach you use from Company X

Dear Name,

Company X is specially inviting you to participate in a study about the types of bleach you use. For your participation in this study you will receive a gift of $XX for your time and feedback.

Please click on the link below to access the survey:

http://website.com/s.asp?ID="Userid"

If you have any questions about the survey, please reply to this email at *studyfocus@vendor.com.*

Thank you for your time and input.

Chapter 7

Sample Sources and Response Rates

There are two primary sampling sources available for research: vendor-provided and proprietary. Vendor-provided samples can be panels or lists of respondents from an outside company. Proprietary sample refers to customer or respondent lists owned by the research sponsor. For vendor-provided samples, the sample usually is sold based on the number of completed surveys. The sample is recruited from sources such as random digit dialing, river sampling, and in some cases, even spyware. Each source has its own advantages and drawbacks and can have dramatically different affects on the results of an online research study. Within these sample sources, the types of respondents can vary widely.

Some sample sources are more effective for online studies than others, especially if the target audience is not online. For example, conducting an online study with young children about the types of business applications they use on their computer, such as spreadsheets, graphics, and word-processing programs, is not appropriate. Panels and lists also may not be the best sample choice for conducting research in specific markets. For example, it can be difficult to conduct online research in a target city because the panel or list becomes too sparse. In this case, a telephone interview or mall intercept would reach the target more effectively. These examples aside, it is generally acceptable to conduct an online study when a large percentage of the audience being studied actively uses the Internet.

Proprietary sample: company customer lists

Surveys can be conducted with proprietary samples. The issue for many companies is first collecting customer email addresses. Many companies now actively ask for customer email addresses along with other standard information such as home address and phone number. Many retailers, like grocers and booksellers, offer reward cards for customers that provide some basic customer information including an email address. Email addresses, which may include both customers and non-customers, can be captured from people visiting the company website.

Assuming that a customer list is available, it is important to understand that responses to surveys completed solely by customers tend to fall into two extremes, either very positive or very negative. This is because most people are not motivated to respond to a survey unless they have an extreme experience. Inviting a broad base of customers that are randomly selected from the email list and sending reminder email invitations to the survey can help increase response rates among customers that have routine experiences. In addition, combining online survey results with customer feedback gathered through telephone interviews can help counter this issue.

A proprietary sample is generally a bit easier to work with than a panel-provided sample. Most of the time, a proprietary sample is tightly governed by the sample owner so there are likely rules already in place to manage privacy, confidentiality, frequency of contact, or other requirements deemed necessary by that particular business. The marketing and legal departments within a company usually understand these predetermined rules. Whenever you use this type of sample, it is important to check with these departments to understand their rules. In many situations, these departments govern the frequency that the list can be contacted because they do not want to over-burden the contacts on the list.

When conducting market research using a proprietary sample, it is important to make respondents aware that their results will not be used for sales and marketing purposes. It must be clear who the owner of the sample list is so that respondents are not concerned about spammers. There are market research organizations, such as Council of American Survey Research Organizations (CASRO), whose bylaws require list owners to use their lists in specific ways for market research purposes.

CASRO rules do allow third-party market research organizations to conduct surveys even if the owner of the sample has not been explicitly granted the right by panel members to be contacted for research purposes. In many proprietary panels, panel members are either added to a list via a sales opportunity or have pre-determined how they would like to be contacted via two different methods:

- Willingness to accept emails from the owner of the list
- Willingness to accept emails from outside companies for offers and other incentives

CASRO has developed a specific certification form for third-party market research companies to provide to their clients when using the client's sample list. It is available at *www.casro.org*.

Some of the important parts of this agreement include:

- A substantive pre-existing relationship exists between the individuals contacted and the research organization, the client, or the list owners contracting the research (the latter being so identified);
- Individuals have a reasonable expectation, based on the pre-existing relationship, that they may be contacted for research;
- Individuals are offered the choice to be removed from future email contact in each invitation; and,
- The invitation list excludes all individuals who have previously taken the appropriate and timely steps to request the list owner to remove them.

The CASRO certification form requires market research companies to fully disclose all relevant information about the owner of the study and purpose of the study. Some organizations even go one step further by requiring that all customer feedback remain anonymous. The benefit of this is that it helps customers ensure their confidentiality and may increase the probability that they will answer the survey questions honestly. The drawback is that follow-up cannot be pursued. These two needs must be weighed before a decision is made. Regardless, the contact should have the right to refuse follow-up within the survey.

As SPAM has become increasingly prevalent on the web, many companies require that their customers opt-in to receive emails from third parties. This issue is especially complex when a market research company is sending emails on behalf of the panel list owner. Generally this opt-in procedure is required to sell the list to third parties and often market research is not considered when the procedures are being established.

Interestingly, market research companies will conduct business and reach out to the panel members on behalf of the company even if the panel members have not explicitly given permission for market research activities. It comes down to whether a market research company will sacrifice business for this fuzzy rule. Technically, the panel members should not be contacted, but when faced with an opportunity to conduct business, it is not so easy to turn down. Treat these situations with caution.

Third-party provided sample

When conducting advertising, brand, product development, or qualitative studies, a third-party provided sample is commonly used because it provides a wider purview of the total market compared with a proprietary sample of the owner's customer base. For these types of research, the audience base being examined generally stretches beyond the current client base to look at competitive threats, opportunities, new ideas from other companies, or detractors of a product or brand. Significant opportunities or challenges could be overlooked with a customer-only based sample whereas third-party provided sample gives companies a view of its competitors or potential future customers.

Online third-party panels have attracted quite a bit of attention compared with panels used for the telephone because they typically have a much lower cost per completed survey. In many situations, the costs of using an online panel can be one-half to two-thirds less than using a telephone-based panel. Additionally, survey responses from online panels can vary from traditional telephone or face-to-face market research. Don Dillman, a University of Washington professor who specializes in market research methods, has shown that survey responses to aurally-directed cues can be quite different than survey responses to visually-directed cues. This issue is addressed in depth later in the sections on multiple-response and scale questions.

Overview of panels

Panels are made up of consumers and business employees that have agreed to be part of an online sample and answer surveys from time to time. To become part of the panel, potential respondents typically must provide basic demographic information that allows the panel company to assert that its panel is representative of the general population. The amount of information a panelist provides can vary widely and can impact what questions need to be included as part of the screening process. Panelists typically receive some sort of incentive for their participation, usually in the form of points that can be accumulated and traded for cash and merchandise.

Panels offer the advantage of not having to screen a lot of people to reach a specific target. Demographic information is already available on respondents, eliminating the need to spend valuable survey time asking those questions. Be sure to ask the panel company how often the demographic information is updated. In addition, many panel companies invite their panelists to complete in-depth surveys on a variety of topics that allow researchers to find hard-to-reach customers such as those with specific financial assets or a health condition. Those that qualify for the survey are the only ones included in the sample.

The primary drawback of using a panel is the concern that the people answering the survey are "professional respondents" and answer many surveys, thus introducing bias into the study. Many panel companies address this issue by instigating business rules that set limits on how many surveys a respondent can answer within a given timeframe and within a given category. This is also balanced with the need to keep panelists engaged by participating in surveys, so there is always an active sample base to draw from. It is important to ask panel companies about their business rules so you can decide if you need further screening criteria. How panel companies deal with this issue is covered in more depth later in this chapter.

Quirk's Marketing Research Review, a market research trade magazine, maintains an excellent directory of market research panels. Quirk's defines its magazine as the marketing research information source for those that conduct, coordinate, and purchase research products and services. The directory of market research panels is global, but it has the heaviest slant towards American panel companies. It can be found at the Quirk's website: *www.quirks.com.*

The tool can easily help a researcher search for panel providers by the specific audience being targeting or type of methodology (e.g., phone, mail, or telephone). It also goes one step further and lists companies that provide proprietary panel management. Some of the companies in this list do not offer access to their panel unless they are used as a full-research service. That is, they must be used to conduct the entire survey, including survey design, questionnaire programming, fielding, data analysis, and reporting. The advantage of Quirk's service is that it provides a few different panel options to choose from. If one source does not provide sample service only, then call the next one on the list.

The following is a list of some of the more common panel providers used in the industry today. These are generally the first-tier providers with the largest panels. There are likely hundreds more panels on the market, especially in niche industries. A simple Internet search using key terms like "market research panels" and the industry or job segment targeted will generate good results. Panel providers include:

comScore	Lightspeed Research
EMI	Market Tools
Gallup	Nielsen
GMI	Research Now
GOL	Schlesinger Associates
Greenfield Online	Survey Sampling International
Harris Interactive	Synovate
Ipsos	The NPD Group
Knowledge Networks	TNS

When selecting a panel provider, consider its strengths. Some panels are better at targeting consumer audiences, some are better at business audiences, and others have only a national focus.

Pricing the panels

When preparing a request for a quote, your request will be expedited if you prepare answers for the following questions:

- Number of waves of the study
- Estimated start date
- Length of screening questionnaire
- Length of questionnaire (not including screener)
- Are there any programming requirements of the panel provider?
- Will personally identifiable information be needed for this study?
- Specific countries needed for the study

- Regions within specific countries
- Definition of the target audience (e.g., business decision-makers within "small" companies—1 to 10 employees)
- Expected *incidence* of the target market (see below)
- Quota targets

Panel incidence

Panel incidence is a tricky discussion in market research. Incidence is defined by the Market Research Association as:

"The frequency of something occurring in the population. It usually refers to persons and is stated as a percentage (i.e., the percentage of people in the U.S. who eat cereal for breakfast). In marketing and opinion research, incidence is a measure of the level of effort needed to reach qualified or eligible respondents."

The tricky part is defining what the population is, a primary input for developing sample costs. For example, when requesting IT decision makers from a technology panel, the incidence would vary dramatically on how the population is defined: the general population, the overall technology market, IT professionals and IT decision makers in a technology-related job, or retailers of technology products. To illustrate, assume a vendor sends out 10,000 invitations to IT decision makers in the U.S.; 1,000 respond, and 400 actually qualify and complete the required part of the survey. The incidence is 40 percent or 400/1,000. In market research, the incidence is the difficulty in reaching the audience. As a purchaser of the sample, you cannot control how many people respond. However, survey screening questions have a rather large impact on the ability to qualify for the survey.

The difficulty in calculating incidence is that it is possible that a portion of the unqualified 600 respondents were not true IT professionals in the first place. They could be business decision makers with some IT functions, but they may not actually function as true IT professionals. This is where the dispute with panel suppliers may begin.

A higher incidence means lower sample costs because the research company will not have to go through as many names to find a qualified respondent and that is reflected in its price quote. Thus, it is important to clarify with the panel provider how it is defining the incidence. Since incidence is typically a required part of a quote request and is also an important factor in determining price, you need to align expectations during the quotation process. Ask the panel provider what it determines the target market to be so that incidence can be calculated accurately. In some cases, both parties may not feel they have an accurate incidence. It is possible to do an incidence check by launching the study with a small proportion of the sample, say 50 to 100 completes, then temporarily shutting the survey down to check the incidence. Cost adjustments can be addressed at this point before the study is put back online.

Panel recruitment approaches

In the early days of online research, panel providers frequently used unscrupulous methods to recruit panelists. Internet surfers were exploited by the use of spyware and their behavior was tracked without any awareness. As people became more aware of their privacy being exploited, laws were passed to prevent this type of unethical panel recruitment.

Today, high-quality panels are recruited from neutral and unbiased sources. For example, a census list of consumers is a good place to start recruiting samples since there is no bias towards a specific audience type. A panel provider who recruits consumers from Coca-Cola sales would not be able to provide an unbiased sample list for other cola products. For business panels, industry census sources such as Dun & Bradstreet are the most credible sources to start from. One of the more common approaches for consumer panels is to use a random digit dial (RDD) method. Basically, an automated dialer starts calling household telephone numbers at random and when someone at the house picks up, an agent is ready to qualify the individual. This is typically one of the more expensive methods because it requires that staff be ready to talk with the potential panelists.

In some situations, panel providers recruit from industry publications. While this is an accepted practice, it is absolutely important to ensure that the publications are not biased towards a specific audience. For example, if you are to survey the software development market in general, it would be unwise to purchase samples for software developers if they were recruited from Linux-based publications. This would result in a biased study.

Contacting a panel provider

When contacting each panel provider it is best to first ask them the breadth and scope before making an inquiry for your specific audience. Ask the panel providers for counts of the panelists by at least the following segments:

- Overall size of the panel
- Country of origin
- Gender
- Job title/description
- Income

Be sure to also ask the focus of their panel. Even though a panel has job descriptions, they may not be particularly strong at gathering a business-related panel. It is important to ask this information prior to submitting a request so that you can avoid the dishonest sales person. Once you are sure that the panel addresses your target market, then you can provide the details for obtaining the costs for the sample you need.

ESOMAR's 25 Panel Questions

The European Society for Opinion and Market Research (ESOMAR) is a global organization dedicated to developing practices and standards to better the market research industry worldwide. The organization has developed a code of professional standards that can be found on their website at *www.esomar.org* within the "About" section under "Professional Standards." All credible panel providers should be able to promptly provide you a response to ESOMAR's list of 25 panel questions. ESOMAR requires that panel providers have the answers to these questions readily available for customers. Any reputable panel provider should consider these questions second nature. While some of them may seem a bit innocuous, they are extremely important. If panel providers cannot give direct and honest answers to these questions, it is best to look for another panel. Do not hesitate to ask panel providers to answer these questions.

1. Is it an actively managed panel (nurtured community) or just a database?

2. Truthfully, how large is it?

3. What is the percentage of "active" members and how are they defined?

4. Where are the respondents sourced from and how are they recruited?

5. Have members clearly opted-in? If so, was this double opt-in?

6. What exactly have they been asked to opt-in to?

7. What do panel members get in return for participating?

8. Is the panel used solely for market research?

9. Is there a privacy policy in place? If so, what does it state?

10. What research industry standards are complied with?

11. Is the panel compliant with all regional, national, and local laws with respect to privacy, data protection and children (e.g., E.U. Safe Harbour), and the Children's Online Privacy Protection Act (COPPA) in the U.S.?

12. What basic socio-demographic profile information, usership, interests data, etc. is kept on members?

13. How often is it updated?

14. In what other ways can users be profiled (e.g., source of data)?

15. What is the (minimum and typical) turn-around time from initial request to first deployment of the emails to activate a study?

16. What are likely response rates and how is response rate calculated?

17. Are or can panel members who have recently participated in a survey on the same subject be excluded from a new sample?

18. Is a response rate (over and above screening) guaranteed?

19. How often are individual members contacted for market research or anything else in a given time period?

20. How is the sample selection process for a particular survey undertaken?

21. Can samples be deployed as batches/replicates, by time zones, geography, etc.? If so, how is this controlled?

22. Is the sample randomized before deployment?

23. Can the time of sample deployment be controlled and, if so, how?

24. Can panel members be directed to specific sites for the survey questionnaire to be undertaken?

25. What guarantees are there to guard against bad data, i.e., respondent cheating or not concentrating/caring in their responses (e.g., click happy)?

Compensating panelists

Each panel provider has its own method of compensating its panelists. Sometimes panel providers offer a quarterly incentive for active participation. Active participation is generally defined as having participated in a certain number of research studies within a specific time period. Others provide points for rewards that can be collected over time and yet others offer a nominal amount per survey completed. Regardless of the approach, it is important to ask the provider how the survey participants will be compensated for your specific study.

Generally the cost of the incentive is embedded in the quote it provides for using its panel, but when you receive a quote, ask if the incentive is included. Depending on how difficult it is to reach the particular audience, a larger incentive may be warranted.

Personally identifiable information from panel providers

Panel providers generally do not permit the collection of Personally Identifiable Information. Not only does it require consent from the respondent, but providing this information also makes the panel provider's business vulnerable to competition. These companies make money by selling the sample over and over. If a person or a company, were able to collect Personally Identifiable Information, they could build their own panels. Panel providers generally require that they review the survey to ensure that this type of information is not collected. Additionally, these companies require contracts that prevent the reuse of their sample without prior consent. Even if it is possible to capture contact information, the legal requirements may be too difficult to overcome.

Professional survey takers

Improper management of incentives could lead to non-random response error in the data set. Basically, cheaters! Many individuals now look at surveys as a method to earn income. Some individuals are also quite good at beating the system, which also suggests that it is important to have an effective screener questionnaire. Reputable panel providers look for ways to more effectively identify and remove these individuals.

Professional survey takers are pervasive in online market research. There are industry publications suggesting that a company announced that 30 percent of its surveys were being taken by only 1 percent of its panelists in 2005 (Bortner, Forrester Research). While its total panel may be representative of the general survey audience, responses to its surveys could be skewed. Professional survey takers are generally identified by:

- Quickness of response to the survey
- Streamlining the survey (picking 1 across all questions)
- Involvement in more than 2 panels
- Inconsistency in expected answers
- Suspicious email address (e.g., using a public email address like hotmail.com in a B2B research study)

It is important to be diligent both in setting up the online survey and reviewing the data set for the study. One effective method to root out cheaters is to ask two similar questions in two slightly different ways. For example, you may ask respondents to rate their satisfaction on a scale of 1 to 10 at the beginning of the survey and then ask them again to rate their satisfaction, but with a yes or no at the end of the survey. The responses should line up.

It is important not to discredit a respondent simply by the response to one question. One must examine the full data set to see if irregularities exist. Be careful in the examination of patterns because you might expect a pattern of positive responses for a legitimately satisfied customer. On the other hand, if the pattern is straight lining, then be cautious and take advantage of the confirmation question outlined in the previous paragraph.

If professional survey takers are identified, in most situations it is best to simply remove them from the data set. This can be costly when every piece of sample counts, but it is also necessary. If the funds are available, other approaches to identifying professional survey takers can include resurveying or doing callbacks. This can be costly, but it can prove to be an effective approach to confirm cheating in the survey and mitigate the impact of non-random response error in the data set.

Beyond Professional Survey Takers: Persuasion from the Sponsoring Company

In David Ensing's article, "How to Address Survey Manipulation by Auto Dealerships" *(Quirk's Marketing Research Review,* October 2008), he focuses on the pervasiveness of another type of cheating that exists in market research. Instead of professional respondents buried inside of panels, auto dealerships may attempt to interfere with the customer satisfaction experience by persuading their customers to fill out surveys that benefit the dealerships. In channel environments such as this one, this can be extremely difficult to manage. It is important to fully disclose the penalties with the channel and conduct a thorough analysis of the data.

Custom panels

The Internet has allowed custom panel development to become more affordable for the average company. It is still not inexpensive by any means, but in some situations it can be done at a relatively affordable price. Almost any reputable market research company will have a team dedicated to building custom panels for its clients. In many situations though, it is simply easier and cheaper to rent from a panel provider as opposed to building your own. If a custom panel is required, consider leveraging the following approaches to make it a little more affordable while maintaining a high level of panel quality.

What are the recruitment methods for the custom panel?

When it comes to panel recruitment you pay for quality. The higher the price, generally the better quality of the panel you receive. The exception of course is harder-to-recruit panelists. However, regardless of costs, it is important to ensure that the recruitment method does not bias the panel layout in a way that is not representative of the market you want to examine. Recruitment can take the form of a census approach or it may be from more targeted lists. Generally, panel providers do not allow you to recruit from their lists, so you have to look for sources that allow you to recruit from their customer list. Many times trade publications are a good source.

Consider various recruitment alternatives and the trade-offs between quality and price when building a custom panel. Pick the model that best fits the needs of your business from both cost and methodological perspectives. Once the panel is set up, it is difficult to change anything—be sure you have thoroughly evaluated the set-up requirements.

What maintenance methods are provided?

Most online custom panel providers offer a full, interactive portal for the participants to use. The portal itself should provide opportunities for the panelists to easily identify the current studies in the field, participate in the research, or even interact with other panelists like a peer-to-peer website. A custom online panel provider should offer more than just panel management. An online portal is relatively inexpensive to build and maintain and the custom online panel provider should already have the framework. The main costs of the custom panel should be initial recruitment and refreshing the panel due to attrition.

A common question to ask with custom panels is "How often should the panel be used?" Like any other research question, it depends. There are several different elements that can affect the answer to this question.

Custom panel incentives

Survey incentives can have a big impact on the rate at which people feel willing to be re-surveyed and the rate at which they will drop out of the panel. Depending on the target audience, a custom panel provider should be able to provide accurate guidance on an appropriate incentive. Generally, harder to find respondents require higher incentives, for example, $25 per survey. Easier-to-find respondents may only require $25 a quarter, or possibly, nothing at all.

Survey frequency for custom panels

Tied directly to survey incentives is the frequency with which the surveys should be conducted. At the very least, a custom panel should be reached at least once a month. Anything more infrequent could lead to higher panel attrition—members may switch jobs, email addresses, forget about the panel, or install new junk-mail filters. Keeping regular and frequent contact is important to prevent panel attrition.

On the flip side, contacting the panelists too often can lead to dissatisfaction and self-removal. There is no consistent rule and it is likely that all custom panel providers will offer their own recommendation, but contacting panelists more frequently than once a week may increase the chance of panelists removing themselves.

Response rates

Inquiring about response rates is very common when renting samples from an online panel provider. Unfortunately, there is rarely a good answer. There are many factors that influence the response rate and the impact that these factors have on response is unknown until the study is actually moved into the field. These factors include:

- Is there an incentive provided?
- Is the target market difficult to recruit (e.g., are you trying to recruit CEOs)?
- Is the survey interesting?
- How long does it take to complete the survey?

River sample

River sampling recruits respondents on the Internet using pop-ups, advertisements, overlays, or any other similar type of capture methods. If a respondent clicks on the specified capture method, then the respondent is screened and assigned to a specified pool of studies for which he or she is qualified to participate. Within the pool of studies, the respondent is randomly assigned to a survey.

While at first blush this would seem to be an appropriate sampling option, there are a few things to beware of. All respondents who end up in the pool of studies are self selected. Self-selected panels are not known to be representative of the studied audience. It is also important to understand the source and breadth of the email addresses. Companies that offer river sampling usually have relationships with a variety of websites that grant them access to intercept an interaction and grab the email address. To ensure a truly representative sample, it is important that the group of websites used attracts a diverse user base in terms of age and gender or are able to target the specific type of respondent needed.

Another issue is the expected completion rate. River sampling does not offer the ability to send out another round of email invitations to fresh respondents as would be the approach if using a panel or customer list and you can end up lingering in-field waiting to finish the last of the completes. Discuss expected completion rates and timing with the sampling company. It should be able to give an accurate estimate as to the required field time needed, with the ability to "widen the river" if necessary, by adding more websites to increase the number of email intercepts.

Many researchers consider river sampling a controversial approach to acquiring samples since the respondents are initially self-selected. They are randomly assigned to the survey, but the act of self-selection at the outset already introduces bias to the respondent set. This does not mean the sample should be ruled out as an option—there may be situations in which it is useful. If an online audience is the target and you can confirm that the characteristics of the sample match the targeted audience, then river sampling may be a good option. In many cases, this sampling approach is cost effective. However, it is important to understand the potential outcome when making an investment of this nature.

Chapter 8

Questionnaire Layout and General Formatting Requirements

The actual layout, format, and appearance of the survey can impact how respondents react and ultimately whether people in an organization credit the survey results. (Survey and Non Response, SuperSurvey Knowledge Base, Ipathia Inc., 2007, *http://knowledge-base.supersurvey. com/survey-response-rate.htm*). Even if a survey is being conducted in a low-cost manner it is important to follow accepted formatting and layout principles to mitigate non-response error. There are some general formatting principles that are not too difficult, but are frequently overlooked when conducting a sound research study. These will help the study to stay on track, maintain its integrity, and legitimize the quality of the output.

Structure: From general to specific questions

Most surveys use the following survey structure:

- Survey Instructions
- Screening questions
- General: company-level questions
- Specific: product-level questions
- Specific: feature-level questions
- Demographics

The goal of the structure above is to ensure that none of the initial questions bias or influence later questions in the survey. One such example is seen in customer satisfaction surveys. Most satisfaction studies start with overall satisfaction with a company or relationship. The study then dives into details around a specific product and possibly a feature of the product. Some people may want to ask about satisfaction with the quality of a specific product feature before asking about satisfaction with the company overall. In this situation, the specific feature question may bias how the respondent feels about the company overall. You might argue that feelings about the company overall can influence how the respondent feels about the specific product features, but if that's the case, then overall company satisfaction will bias all of the other specific product features equally. Asking about the specific product feature at the beginning will bias overall company satisfaction and then an accurate comparison against all product features will be difficult, especially if everything is out of order.

First Step: Instructions at the beginning of a survey

It is generally advised to provide instructions to the respondent at the beginning of a study. This helps respondents understand the purpose of the study, whether an incentive will be provided, and to assure them that it is for research purposes only. There are many fraudulent organizations scamming people into thinking they are responding to a survey, but are actually capturing personal information for financial gain. In the instructions, it is important to state the following:

- The organization conducting the survey
- Either the sponsoring company, or the research company hosting the survey
- The actual survey objective
- If an incentive is being provided
- The estimated time to complete the study
- That the study is a "market research" study

Second Step: Body of the survey

The body of the survey should take on a flow of general to specific. It is important that preceding questions do not bias the questions that follow in a survey. This can discredit the entire survey and risk the money paid for the services already rendered. Market research companies definitely will not provide a refund nor will the online survey tool companies.

Typically, the high-level or company-oriented questions begin a survey. These are followed by product-specific questions, and then proceed to feature-level specific questions. Where a trade-off analysis occurs and there is no hierarchy in the study, it is important to think about the impact that a question will have on subsequent questions—an initial question should not bias a subsequent question.

Third Step: Finalizing the survey

Unlike an essay or a story where the conclusion reaches a climax or proves a hypothesis, the final part of the survey should contain the least critical information to the study objectives. Generally, the end of the survey should request demographic or other information that is less critical to meeting the objective of the survey. The questions at the end should contain information that allows the organization to analyze other questions in the survey.

Consumer-oriented surveys

For consumer-oriented surveys, most of the demographics questions are likely to be about income, age, gender, work status, or ethnicity. These are only placed at the end of the survey if they are not critical to qualification of the study or for critical analysis.

Business-oriented surveys

Business-oriented surveys that contact business managers or workers can have a wide variety of question types at the end. Many times the questions are relevant to the specific business. For example, in business-oriented studies the questions at the end of the survey may cover job title, industry, decision-making authority, length of employment, or number of employees in the organization.

The questions at the end of the study should be considered "Nice to Haves" not "Need to Haves."

Survey formatting

The manner in which questions are formatted can impact how a respondent reacts to the questions. In some cases respondents may even exit the survey early if the respondent experience becomes too burdensome. There are some basic rules to consider around the formatting of studies.

Using a banner to brand a survey

If a company is identified in a study (i.e., a non-blind study), it is recommended that a banner image of the company logo be inserted at the top of every survey page. The Internet hosts plenty of scams and adding a banner helps ensure confidence in the study's legitimacy. Generally, companies with an online site have a standard banner or graphic that can be inserted easily into online sites or other company material. Ask marketing communications or public relations staff for an appropriate graphic.

Using color elements

Using colors to depict emotions or characterize levels of satisfaction is one of the biggest mistakes in poor quality surveys. Interpretations of color can have significant differences across cultures. For example, red means stop in the U.S., but in China, it represents a very positive emotion. You might ask, "Can I use colors in a country-specific survey?" It is generally recommended that colors not be used—entire countries rarely have an unmixed cultural background today. When conducting a study in nearly any highly-populated metropolitan area in the world, the respondent base is likely to cross a wide variety of ethnicities.

One example commonly seen in market research surveys is applying colors to scales. In the U.S. or UK you might see red, yellow, and green blending across a scale. Red would be applied to the negative end of the scale, yellow to the neutral or middle part, and green to the positive end—the familiar traffic signal arrangement. But again, this scale is not universally accepted across all cultures.

Colors should be used only when there is a very specific need and target market to test. There are exceptions to all rules and trade-offs to make, but understanding that colors can be interpreted differently across divergent cultures mitigates any potential misuse.

Background colors

Some people might find a plain white survey background a little boring, but research should never be turned into a marketing effort. Generally, survey tools use one solid color as a background, typically white, a light grey, or a soft blue. The color of the background should be soft to the eyes and not overpowering. If at any point a marketing message is conveyed or if the background distracts respondents, then the integrity of the survey is questioned. Do not let the background color overpower the survey questions.

Text styles

Microsoft Office, Open Office, and even Google documents now offer a wide variety of text styles and fonts. As survey platforms evolve, research organizations are constantly looking for ways to improve how survey text actual appears. Here are both some general etiquette rules to follow and also text styles to incorporate into the survey.

Text etiquette: capital letters and acronyms

Capital letters are often used to emphasize a point, but on the

Internet, they are commonly interpreted as a form of anger. It is recommended to avoid capital letters in questionnaires or survey invitations. For example, if you request that a questionnaire be completed ASAP, respondents may find that irritating and avoid the survey. Or worse, it could impact survey results due to non-response error.

An acronym is an abbreviation for a longer phrase. In all industries and companies, there are acronyms that are commonly used among a group of individuals or organizations. However, it is not safe to assume that everyone knows what all acronyms mean. It is generally advised not to use jargon because some respondents will not be familiar with the specific acronym.

Text etiquette: bold, italics, and underlines

Bolding words or phrases must be used cautiously as it can be interpreted differently. While the intention may be to stress or emphasize a point, bolding could easily be misinterpreted as implying a positive or negative emotion. All surveys should maintain a level of objectivity; if objectivity is maintained, bolded words or phrases can be used. But like most other types of specialized formatting, bolding is discouraged. Bolding can be used in rare cases when trying to emphasize a point.

Italicized words have a similar impact as bolded words on the respondent, except they generally convey a little less emphasis. Italics can be used in the same situations that bolding can, but once again, it is important to use them cautiously and sparingly.

Underlining words is similar to bolded and italicized words. The underline can stress a particular point being made, but should be used with caution as it can be interpreted in a negative fashion.

Text etiquette: combining various formatting

Even more critical than using one of the above formatting techniques is the impact of combining them. Bolding, italicizing, and underlining all have the general effect of emphasizing a point. Combining these techniques increases their effect on the point you're trying to make. While this use of formatting is seen in surveys, even greater caution must be exercised because it could further bother or distract respondents.

Common font styles

There are a variety of font styles being used in online surveys. Generally it does not matter which font is used as long as it is used consistently. Two of the older, more commonly used fonts are *Arial* and *Times New Roman*. Both are adequate, but a little dated. Since Office 2007 was introduced, more survey tools incorporate softer-looking fonts such as *Calibri*. Stay away from elaborate or difficult to-read-fonts—use a straightforward-looking font with few enhancements.

Except under rare circumstances, do not use the same font that the hosting company uses to market or brand its product or service. The font style of the brand could be used in customer satisfaction surveys, but keep in mind the potential bias this could create with customers (or respondents). If brand's font is replicated, it alone could bias the responses, even in a customer satisfaction survey. Respondents may have a predisposition to the brand. They could interpret the survey questions in the manner in which they feel about the brand. Bias is introduced and with it, skepticism of the survey results.

Page breaks

Page breaks are also known as screen breaks. The terms are used interchangeably in online research. Page breaks can be quite tricky since they are generally used for two reasons: to accommodate branching or skip logic that requires visual breaks between the questions, or to prevent a list of questions from appearing too long.

The point at which the survey questions bifurcate is where a page break occurs. Most surveys have some skip logic among questions that require a segment of the population to answer questions specific to the relationship, work, or type of classification they belong to. For example, you might ask a different set of questions to a 21-

year-old than a 50-year-old. Therefore, the questions may start with age—those who are 21 would answer one set of questions while the older group would answer a different set of questions.

Another reason to use page breaks is when the list of questions displayed on the screen appears too long. A long list can contribute to respondent fatigue. When the list appears shorter respondent, fatigue is likely to be less. This has a critical impact on survey incidence, and ultimately drives down costs because fewer respondents will need to be recruited to achieve adequate sample sizes.

Referencing outside information

Survey makers commonly ask themselves, "Should we reference website X and have respondents leave the survey to view the information?" In most situations it is best not to have them leave the survey. Each time respondents leave the survey, it gives them the opportunity not to come back. Researchers generally agree that the information should be contained within the survey. There are different survey tools and methodologies that allow researchers to put the necessary information inside the survey tool. For example, a discrete choice or conjoint analysis is a technique in which sets of information can be compared against each other. Images, marketing collateral, and so forth are contained within these tools.

If a set of information is being evaluated and needs to be contained within the tool, ensure that the survey tool contains the capabilities to do so. Simple techniques, such as copying a screen image, can negate the need to refer to an outside site. If a person is referred to an outside site and leaves the survey, incidence is likely to worsen. If at all possible, try to keep all of the information contained within the survey so that nothing distracts respondents from completing the survey process.

There are a few exceptions to the rules, of course. If a privacy policy or other legal information cannot be contained within a survey, then it is generally acceptable to reference the outside source.

However, this still could contribute to incomplete survey responses. From a practical standpoint, it is unlikely that many people will actually read the privacy policy or legal information so the impact on respondents is likely to be negligible. The best case scenario is to keep this information within the survey while allowing respondents to easily continue the survey process. To appease lawyers, you may be forced to handle legal documentation a certain way. While costs may be impacted if respondents leave the survey, if a lawyer requires this information to be displayed, then it is likely to save you money in the long term and prevent you from encountering any unnecessary legal claim.

It is generally all right to reference a privacy policy outside the survey. It is generally not all right to references images outside of the survey site.

The concern with visual displays is that they can be very costly. Sometimes marketing departments have already created visual concepts that simply need to be tested. If so, the costs are obviously low. If not, development teams sometimes need to be assembled to create the images or production teams for videos.

Chapter 9

Survey Programming Rules

Instead of generalizing questions or conducting multiple surveys across different segments of the survey population, programming logic can permit the survey maker the flexibility to build questions specific to certain respondent populations. This type of programming is known to market researchers because these techniques have long been used in telephone research. In telephone research, interviewers use a computer-based tool that moves from screen to screen as the interviewer inputs the respondents' answers. The difference between traditional telephone programming rules and online programming rules is that respondents see everything in the online tool and they are not aided by an individual in the survey process.

Since the respondent sees everything in a research tool, it is best to insert enough programming rules so that the survey appears as customized as possible. This permits a level of specificity that is tailored to each respondent. The drawback is that the level of specificity could be wrong. Keeping it general may minimize errors, but it may not also be specific enough to answer the research and business objectives.

Three primary types of programming rules are:

- **Autofills:** Lets the survey maker insert words specific to each respondent
- **Branching rules or skip logic:** Lets the survey maker target a specific set of questions for each respondent

- **Order rotations:** A set of attributes or questions can be auto-matically rotated in an ordered or unordered fashion

Autofills

Autofill is a powerful programming capability that allows the survey maker the ability to populate specific words into a question. The following is a simple example of how Autofills are used:

How many personal computers (PCs) has your organization purchased in the last year?

_____# of PCs (insert number)

– – – – – – – – – – – – – – PAGE BREAK – – – – – – – – – – – – – –

Of the <Insert Answer from Q1> personal computers that your organization purchased within the last year, what percent are laptops?

_____% laptops (insert number)

This is an autofill programming rule. The number of PCs from the first question was inserted into the second question to help the respondent determine the percent of laptops in his organization overall. Notice that a page break was used to separate the questions. Without the page break, the autofill cannot be used. The advantage of this type of programming rule is that the second question reminds the respondent of the exact number of PCs inserted in the first question. Question two could have been phrased "What percent of your total PCs are laptops?" But if there is a page break between the questions, the respondent could forget what he inserted in the first question. Data fills help ensure a little more accuracy in the survey.

Branching rules

Branching rules allow respondents to skip to various questions in the survey depending on their qualifications, either through predetermined information gathered in the sample acquisition process or through direct questions in the survey. The terms skip logic and branching rules are used interchangeably since they mean and do the same thing. It is really a matter of preference to the organization using it.

The following is a flow diagram outlining the process when a branching rule is used:

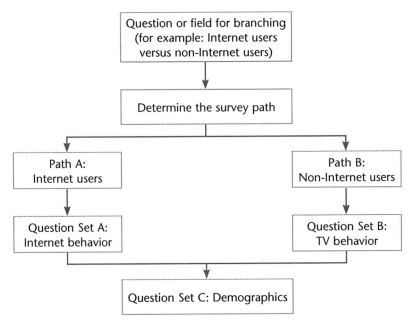

At the first step of a branching rule, either a question or a predetermined field must be set to establish the criterion that determines the set of questions a respondent will see. Each question set will then be asked of the appropriate respondent. If needed, at the conclusion of each question set, the respondents may be grouped back together and all asked the same questions. In the diagram above, demographics is used as the final set of questions that both sets of respondents will answer.

If needed, the questionnaire can branch into multiple sets or even sub-sets. Keep in mind that the more often a study branches into multiple sections, the more you should be concerned with the available sample size for the segment, or sub-segment. In survey development, business needs may push for very specific questions, but this must be balanced with survey complexity and costs. Branching can have a large impact on sample costs but at the same time if the detail is not provided, there may be skepticism about the survey data. It is a delicate balancing act of trade-offs. There is no perfect solution, but the trade-offs must be managed in a way that satisfies the business needs and mitigates costs.

Branching rules with data fill

In many cases branching rules and data fill rules must be combined. Most survey tools can, and should, handle this level of complexity. The following example incorporates both branching rules and data fill rules.

Here, the type of Internet connection and frequency of use is explored. The example assumes the respondent already has an Internet connection.

1a. Which of the following best describes the type of Internet connection you have at your home?

- ○ 56k telephone modem Internet connection
- ○ DSL Internet connection
- ○ Cable Internet connection
- ○ Fiber optic Internet connection
- ○ T1/T3 Internet connection
- ○ Other

– – – – – – – – – – – – – PAGE BREAK – – – – – – – – – – – – –

Programming Rules:
<If Q1 = f, then ask Q1b.>

1b. How would you describe the type of Internet connection you have at your home?

Please specify:_____

------------ PAGE BREAK ---------------

Programming Rules:
<If Q1 = a, b, c, d, e then ask Q2a. If Q1 = f, then ask Q2b.>

2a. For your ***<Insert answer from Q1>***, how many days a week do you use it?

  ○ One day a week

  ○ 2 – 3 days a week

  ○ 4 – 5 days a week

  ○ 6 – 7 days a week

2b. For your Internet connection, how many days a week do you use it?

  ○ One day a week

  ○ 2 – 3 days a week

  ○ 4 – 5 days a week

  ○ 6 – 7 days a week

The actual type of Internet connection the respondent selected in question 1 is inserted into question 2a. This allows respondents to think about the specific type of Internet connection in regards to their weekly use. Question 2b does not provide any level of specificity because the response gathered from previous questions was "Other" and a fill-in-the-blank. Since question 1b could be left empty, it is best not to specify the Internet connection in question 2. You could require respondents to answer question 1b, but the answer they provide may not be clean or even legible. Given the potential responses to question 1b, it is probably best to use the generic question in 2b as the follow up to question 1b.

In this example, both data fills and branch rules have been used.

The goal is to display questions that are appropriate for the respondents based on the answers they provided in the survey. Branching rules and data fills are powerful tools that improve the survey experience, drive data accuracy, and bring legitimacy to the survey output.

Order rotations

In many surveys, respondents are asked to rate a set of questions or statements based on a scale. For simplicity, these will be called *attributes*. In some cases the attributes listed in a specific order may cause a bias in the responses and some of the answers may be skewed because of attributes seen previously in the survey. A method to deal with this is to randomly rotate the order of the attributes.

While there is no consistent rule, when at least three or four questions or statements are listed it is important to consider randomly rotating them. It is not necessary to do this, but it should be considered. Rotation may not be necessary if there is a natural flow of the statements or questions that reflect the natural environment in which the relationship or experience occurs, but sometimes the questions or statements are not dependent on each other.

For example, consider rating the following attributes on a satisfaction scale of 0 to 10.

- Quality of technical support
- Quality of customer service
- Ease of doing business
- Quality of the product
- Quality of the salesperson

The five attributes listed can be displayed to the respondent in any order. However, if a person called the technical support line and had a bad experience, he would likely end up rating technical support poorly. It is then possible that his reaction to seeing the technical support attribute could influence how he responds to the other attributes. While a respondent may be able to rate the attributes independently, it is best to randomly rotate them so that this effect is mitigated. With enough survey completes, the impact of this ordering is minimized since this effect will be naturally distributed across the entire sample.

Not all surveys tools have this capability, so before any money is spent with a research organization or a survey tool, investigate whether it is available.

Chapter 10

Single-Punch and Multi-Punch Questions

Two of the more common types of research questions are single-punch and multi-punch. Single-punch questions allow respondents to select one response per question. Multi-punch questions allow respondents to select as many responses as are available in a question. Technology also enables researchers to ask an "in-between" question. That is, a respondent can select a specified number of answers. For example, select the top three. Another example is when a respondent can select a specified answer as well as an "Other: please specify." It is important to understand the differences in these types of questions as they each have strong differences on the results as they are applied to the business.

Creating a question

Sometimes you get stuck trying to properly formulate a question. The easiest thing to do is simply type the business question or need into a word-processing document. Think of it as free-flowing writing. This helps to prevent writer's block. If no ideas are popping up, post your thoughts on a social forum. Even asking friends on Facebook may provide helpful ideas. The ironic thing is that once the idea is posted on a social networking site, the idea was just typed. Do not worry about the precise wording of the question at this point, because you should review the question once the answers have been written.

At the start of writing the question, only worry about getting the question written down.

Starting with a very simple question, you could ask, "Where do you like to go Snow Skiing?" The second stage is to provide a list of answers. For example:

Where do you like to go snow skiing?

○ Squaw Valley

○ Alpine Meadows

○ Vail

○ Breckenridge

○ Other

The initial question and answer set have been formulated. It is now important to review the question and answer set to determine if the set has been appropriately, and correctly, created. An effective method to validate the correctness of the question is to think about it from a respondent perspective.

If a respondent looks at this question his first reaction may be to select as many of the answers that apply. However, the author of the question may have really wanted respondents to select the primary location at which they prefer to ski. In this case, it is probably worth rewording to something like, "At which of the following resorts do you prefer to go snow skiing?" This would require that respondents have the ability to select only one of the responses as opposed to multiple responses. It is easy to distinguish the difference between the multi-punch answer set and the single-punch answer set.

Now that the question has been rephrased, a final review of the answer set must be completed. Only four resorts are listed above, but there are many more locations all over the world. It is perfectly acceptable to have a reduced list, but it is also important to ensure that is it targeted to the respondent base. If this question were fielded in Italy, the resorts should be replaced by slopes with which Italians are most familiar. As the study becomes increasingly complex due to translations or other international components, it may be more cost-effective to sub-contract to a research company able to execute the study.

Single-punch guidelines

A single-punch question should be created so that a respondent can select only one response per question. There must be at least two answers (for example, yes or no), but there is theoretically no upper limit on the number of answers. We recommend capping the number of answers between 10 to 15 to prevent respondent fatigue, but the list can be longer if absolutely required. If it is longer, alternative approaches are recommended (see "Long answer lists" below). There are a few different techniques that should be employed to ensure respondents understand the difference between multi-punch and single-punch questions. They include:

- Visual layout and technical implementations
- Question semantics
- Stated requirements

The visual display and technical implementations of single-punch answers

There is a stark difference in the use of single-punch versus multi-punch answer sets. Single-punch answers are typically denoted with open circles. Referring back to the snow skiing question, the answer set has bullets with open circles. The open circles become checked or filled in once a respondent has selected a specific option.

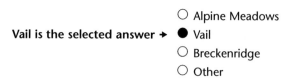

The visual layout of the bullets must function so that if another option is selected, the first selected option will become unchecked and the new one checked. Most platforms switch the selected button from the first selected option to the second selection option if the respondent tries to make multiple selections. Additionally, the technical elements of the survey platform must prohibit a person from selecting multiple answers in a single-answer type question. If the capability does not exist in the technical platform, then it may be time to find another survey platform altogether.

The standards denoted here are most commonly seen in the industry, but there are customized survey platforms that employ their own standards. As an industry, it is most beneficial for researchers to standardize a single approach because this makes the respondent survey interaction consistent. The consistency permits comparability research and makes all output much more useful.

Question semantics

The manner in which a question is phrased has a critical impact in giving respondents proper guidance to answer the survey questions. For example, a direction stated as, "Please select the responses that best describe your personality," assumes that a person will be able to select multiple responses. If this question were employed in a survey, but the respondent was given the option to select only one answer, this wording might lead to confusion—the question and directions are contradictory. Too much confusion in a survey can lead to respondent fatigue and too much respondent fatigue leads to the higher costs associated with uncompleted surveys. Aligning the question semantics with the technical implementation ensures the respondent has a good survey experience.

Stated requirements

The third technique to employ is to use stated directions in the question. Once again looking at the snow skiing question, here is an example:

At which of the following resorts
do you prefer to go snow skiing?

Clearly stated direction →   *(Please select only one)*

The direction, "Please select only one" is clearly labeled. Other phrases commonly used include:

- Select one
- Select only one
- Please select one response
- Please select only one response
- Check one only

It is generally recommended that a cordial request be used. It does not hurt to use a friendly "please" in the directions. Also, use of italics helps to emphasize the requirement. These directions clearly provide respondents the specific directions to select only one response. In case the question is not phrased correctly, the directions remove any ambiguity in how many answers a respondent is able to select.

Multi-punch guidelines

Multi-punch questions require that respondents select as many answers as they wish. This type of question is used in many scenarios—to assess behaviors, attitudes, preferences, usage, and many more. The following example is a common type of question to understand behaviors:

Which of the following activities do you do while surfing the web? *(Please select all that apply)*

☐ Talk on IM
☐ Interact on social networking sites like Facebook
☐ Conduct business
☐ Buy and sell
☐ Blog
☐ Research
☐ Keep track of the news

This question asks respondents to identify all of the different activities that they do while on the web. It provides a pre-defined list that requires the respondents to select from the answers provided.

While there could be other answers not identified in this list, this type of question helps guide respondents to provide an answer to a specified list.

The visual display and technical implementations of multi-punch answers

In contrast to single-punch answers, multi-punch answers are generally denoted by the use of open boxes at the beginning of the answer. As respondents select the responses, the boxes are generally placed with an "x" in the middle of the box.

	☐ Answer 1
Answer 2 and ➜	☒ Answer 2
	☐ Answer 3
Answer 4 are selected in this example ➜	☒ Answer 4

All survey platforms should employ this technology as it is one of the most common and basic survey questions used in market research. In fact, this question type has proven to be especially helpful for online surveys versus telephone surveys because the list is shown in its entirety as opposed to being read one by one. When lists are long, it is not uncommon for phone respondents to either forget a specific response that was read to them, or object to the time taken for the entire list to be read. Online implementation has proven to be a significant cost savings due to the reduced survey length. This provides an opportunity to create additional questions.

Question semantics

The methods in which multi-punch questions are written are slightly different from single-punch questions. The goal is to inform respondents that they will have the ability to select multiple boxes. Common types of questions or statements include:

- Please select the options . . .
- Which of the following . . . ?
- Which of the statements describe . . . ?

- Please check the answers that most align to your perceptions of Company X.
- Please indicate which of the following functions your company commonly uses.
- Please select all of the responses that . . .
- What are the reasons for deploying "x" technology in your company?
- Which information sources do you rely on for your international news?

Typically, a multi-punch question avoids words that require a respondent to select one response. The words are generally singular in nature. These words include:

- Best
- Primary
- Favorite
- First
- Most

Stated requirements

The third element to properly structure a multi-punch question is to provide a stated direction. This direction must easily and clearly tell respondents that they can select as many of the answers as they feel appropriate. Many commonly used statements include:

- Please check all that apply
- Please select all that apply
- Please check all that are applicable

It is good practice to be courteous in stated directions. Avoiding courteous words may lead to dissatisfaction with the survey experience. The extra few words added to the survey will have a negligible cost impact. Using "please" and "thank you" should be common practice in survey research. Respondents are critical to research success; it is not worth offending them.

The "in-between" questions

Many survey platforms provide the opportunity to "select 3" or "rank 3" from a larger set of multi-punch answers. This is a slightly more customized version of a survey tool, but it is a feature that most survey tools should provide. This requirement is common among researchers as it is an easy method to gather stated rankings.

There are a few common approaches to limiting multi-punch questions. For "select 3," a commonly used approach is a multi-punch (e.g., *Select all that apply*) question, but the software limits the user to selecting only three different boxes.

For a ranking question, there are two different options. The first is to provide a single list with an open box next to each answer. Respondents are directed to fill in the appropriate number that matches their ranking. The following shows how the question can be displayed:

Please rank three activities that you most commonly do on the Internet. *(Please rank the top three)*

_____ Talk on IM

___1__ Interact on social networking sites like Facebook

_____ Conduct business

___3__ Buy and sell

_____ Blog

___2__ Research

_____ Keep track of the news

The disadvantage of this approach is that it requires respondents to write in a response. Generally, respondents have an easier time checking boxes as opposed to writing in responses. Checking boxes limits any kind of error in the survey. Some survey tools do have the capability to limit text inputs to only numeric digits and can also require that at least three responses be ranked. However, requiring responses may frustrate survey respondents and may lead to respondents dropping out of the survey.

Another example of ranking is to provide check boxes in a grid format. This approach limits any kind of error due to write-in responses, but requires respondents to review the different columns in order to properly rank the attributes. The following is an example of a check-box based ranking question:

Please rank three activities that you most commonly do on the Internet. *(Please rank the top three, select one response per column)*

	Top activity	2nd activity	3rd activity
Talk on IM	○	○	○
Interact on social networking sites like Facebook	○	○	●
Conduct business	●	○	○
Buy and sell	○	○	○
Blog	○	○	○
Research	○	●	○
Keep track of the news	○	○	○

In the example above, "Conduct business" is ranked as the top activity, "Research" is ranked as the second activity, and "Interact on social network sites like Facebook" is ranked as the third activity. It is a bit more cumbersome for respondents to align all of the columns with each row, but it does eliminate some of the error associated with written responses. Either approach will get the job done and there is generally no difference in costs. At a minimum, ensure that the survey platform being used provides at least one of the two options.

Long answer lists

Long answer lists create a problem for researchers regardless of the survey medium being used. The longer the answer lists become, the more likely respondents will become fatigued and exit the study. As more respondents exit the study, research costs begin to rise because more samples must be purchased to obtain completed surveys. Online survey tools provide a few useful options, but each option has different drawbacks.

Tree questions

One approach to mitigating the effect of lengthy answer lists is to start general and then get specific. For example, a large consumer packaged goods company may want to know all of the brands of cigarettes people smoke in emerging markets. To start, there are some brands that people are familiar with. However, many may not be familiar with the specific brands of cigarettes available in each country. Given that there are likely 10 to 30 different cigarette companies, each with a few hundred brands, the lists must be broken out. Start general, then move to specific. The first question should ask which brands they smoke at a high level. Then, in the follow-up questions, respondents will be shown only responses relevant to the cigarette company selected in the first question. If a respondent does not select Camel, then there is no point in showing any of the Camel brands in subsequent questions. This saves space in the survey and allows the researcher to open up other space for additional use.

To do this effectively, branching logic must be used (see Chapter 9). Branching logic prevents the respondent from seeing questions that are irrelevant. Each survey platform will have its own programming for generating branching logic. As long as it is available and its logic is easy to implement, tree questions can be built easily within surveys.

It is important to stay away from survey platform vendors who claim they could build this technology for a fee. Not only should this be a required feature of their tool, but if they build it, they will surely deploy it across all of their research on your dime. Tell them you want royalties for each time the technology is deployed in subsequent research efforts. That will help to negotiate price.

Chapter 11

Using Grid or Matrix Questions

Grid questions are used frequently in online research to lay out questions that are asked the same way. This approach enables respondents to go through a group of questions quickly. It works well with attribute ratings and agreement statements, as well as check lists. The advantage to respondents is that they can answer multiple questions when it appears to look like only one question. This might have some influence on a more positive survey experience and also shorten the length of the questionnaire. These types of questions are good at stretching the ability to gather more information in a timely manner. This in turn should create better value as a richer set of data will result.

Advantage of grid questions in a web survey

In a more traditional phone survey, interviewers are typically required to restate the scale as a person on the phone may forget what the scale represents. The advantage of a web survey is that the performance scales can be stated once at the beginning of the section, then laid out in a manner which respondents can easily remember and reference. This quickens the respondent experience and can either shorten overall survey length or permit you to add additional questions.

Listing ratings and attributes in columns and rows

Some of the examples provided below have the rating points across the top and the attributes listed across the side. Some might suggest that rating points and attributes be flipped so that the points are on the side and attributes across the top. Researchers will generally advise against flipping the axes, because there is limited space in the cells across the top of the grid. In a web page, there is a limited amount of space in which the grid can be displayed moving from left to right across the screen. Web surfers are quite familiar with scrolling up and down on a screen, but they generally do not move left to right. Anything displayed in the horizontal axis should fit within an 800x600 pixel screen resolution. This is a smaller screen resolution, but one that will work with a large portion of all web surfers, including those in emerging markets.

Length of attribute lists

Keeping the attributes listed in the columns technically enables you to list as many attributes as needed. However, the larger the list, the more cumbersome it appears to the respondent. It is not only important to consider the actual time to get through the list, but that the appearance of a large list may dissuade respondents from completing the survey. A general rule of thumb is: keep the list to no more than 15 attributes. If a longer list is needed, then you should consider entering a page break and restarting the list and directions on a subsequent page.

Grid: Scale questions

In the scale grids listed below, a 1 to 5 scale is used. This is not intended to recommend it as the ideal scale to use in a grid, rather it was chosen arbitrarily. There are some effects to using larger scales in grid questions that have an impact on screen width, but the actual scale length should be chosen for a multitude of other reasons that are covered in Chapter 13.

Performance scale

In this first example, respondents are asked to rate a set of statements based on how they think a specific brand performs. As the directions state, a higher score represents better performance, a lower score represents lower performance. Respondents are asked to rate each row on the 1 to 5 scale. The directions, which are just below the respondent request to rate the attributes, ask the respondent to select one rating per row. Radio buttons are typically used in this type of grid question.

Using a scale from "1" to "5" where "5" is "excellent" and "1" is "poor" please rate detergent Brand A on the following attributes. *(Please check one per row)*

	1	2	3	4	5
Cleans grass stains	○	○	○	○	○
Leaves clothes smelling fresh	○	○	○	○	○
Value for the money	○	○	○	○	○

Agreement scale

An agreement scale is an additional option to gathering respondent feedback. It is similar to a performance scale, but differs in the stated respondent request and potentially the manner in which the attributes are stated. It is merely an alternative option to performance scales that are commonly used in grid questions. A respondent is still required to select one response per row and radio buttons are typically used.

Using a scale from "1" to "5" where "5" is "Strongly agree" and "1" is "Strongly disagree" please rate detergent Brand A on the following attributes.

(Please check one per row)

	1	2	3	4	5
Is a brand I trust	○	○	○	○	○
Is an environmentally safe brand	○	○	○	○	○
Is worth what I pay for it	○	○	○	○	○

Grid: Single-punch questions

Single-punch questions embedded into grids are similar to scale questions inside of grids. The only difference is that the numerical codes running horizontally, or across the top, have specific answers. An example of a single-punch question is provided below.

When do you plan to begin using the following technologies?

(Please check one per row)

	I already do	In 6 months	In 6-12 months	In 12-24 months	Greater than 2 years
The Internet	○	○	○	○	○
Email on your mobile phone	○	○	○	○	○
A SaaS* customer relations solution	○	○	○	○	○

*Software as a Service

Grid: Check lists

Check lists within grids can get quite complex and difficult for respondents. As the complexity increases, the chance that someone makes a mistake in the survey increases. However, check list grids do provide researchers the ability to combine multiple questions to save time and space.

Check-list grids allow respondents to select multiple answers by row or column. The complexity for respondents arises because it is difficult to remember and differentiate the rows and columns. Within check-list grids, it is especially important to have every other row highlighted with a light background color so that respondents can easily track the attribute to which they are responding. It is also important that the attributes be listed in the rows on the left of the table and a limited number of items be listed across the top, or columns. This minimizes confusion due to the magnitude of the request. Remember to keep the grid as simple and clear as possible, while trying to maximize as much space as possible. Example:

Below is a list of attributes that may or may not describe the brands shown. For each attribute, please check the brand or brands that are associated with the attribute.

(Please check all that apply)

	Brand A	Brand B	Brand C	All Brands	None of these Brands
Uses natural ingredients	O	O	O	O	O
An expert in children's products	O	O	O	O	O
Has products that are dye-free	O	O	O	O	O

Rotation of the attribute list in grids

It is important to keep respondents in mind when designing grid questions because it is easy to overload them. Lists should be randomly rotated to avoid response bias. However, if a brand list is being evaluated, it is best to keep that consistent as respondents tend to look at a brand list and then assume the brands will remain in the same position.

If a list of attributes or statements is very long, it can be broken up into blocks of attributes/statements that appear on a page. If this approach is used, the best practice is to randomly rotate attributes within the block and randomly rotate the blocks. This can be cumbersome for programmers, so in practice blocks may be rotated based on a predefined rule or not at all. Another programming solution is to create several versions of the questionnaire with the block placement already set. This ensures a specific number of respondents see the block of attributes in a certain order, which is different than another group of respondents as the example below demonstrates.

Building a rotation scheme

To build a block rotation, you first need to consider the number of variables to be rotated and the sample size. The idea is to break the attributes into blocks of attributes (i.e., Block 1 = Attributes 1–5, Block 2 = Attributes 6–10, etc.) and then break the sample into groups such that each attribute block is evaluated in the first position by a sub-segment of the sample. As an example, assume a 20-attribute list and sample size of 400 completes. A simple block rotation might look like the table below. Each block contains five attributes and each of the four blocks appears in first position to be evaluated by a portion of the sample. The sample is divided into four groups and each group gets a different version of the questionnaire that includes a different version of the block rotation. The order of those five variables is randomly rotated within each block. Respondent-level data would need to include which version of the survey respondents had so the data could be properly aggregated. The versions could be created with each of the assignments in the table below. This assignment establishes equal preference to each of the blocks. Theoretically, any bias affects due to Block 1 being answered first would be mitigated by the rotation scheme since all blocks will share preference across the entire respondent base.

Version 1	Version 2	Version 3	Version 4
Block 1	Block 2	Block 3	Block 4
Block 2	Block 3	Block 4	Block 1
Block 3	Block 4	Block 1	Block 2
Block 4	Block 1	Block 2	Block 3

In addition, each time a block is presented, the anchor—the horizontal information, should be repeated consistently for the respondent as shown in the example below.

Q. Please indicate which brands are associated with the following attributes.

(Please check all that apply)

	Brand A	Brand B	Brand C
Block 1			
Attribute 1	○	○	○
Attribute 2	○	○	○
Attribute 3	○	○	○
Attribute 4	○	○	○
Attribute 5	○	○	○

	Brand A	Brand B	Brand C
Block 2			
Attribute 6	○	○	○
Attribute 7	○	○	○
Attribute 8	○	○	○
Attribute 9	○	○	○
Attribute 10	○	○	○

Chapter 12

Open-Ended Questions

Open-ended questions are great tools to collect respondents' feedback in an unstructured manner. Open-ended questions conducted online often generate more productive content than telephone interviews because respondents are more likely to censor their comments for the interviewer. In addition, respondents do not have the time pressure associated with telephone surveys when an interviewer is trying to complete the survey within a specific time to keep the cost per interview down.

However, open-ended questions should be used judiciously within a survey because they can eat up time. On average, it takes the typical respondent 15 to 30 seconds to type in a thoughtful response. In addition, too many open-ended questions can annoy respondents and may lead to one-word answers or skipping the question altogether as they move through the survey. Examples of where open-ended questions can be very beneficial are outlined below.

Follow-up to scale questions

Open-ended questions can be used to follow up on a scale question to provide insight into a rating, particularly if the rating is either very positive or very negative.

Q1. Now, we'd like to understand your feelings about Company A overall. Please rate your overall satisfaction with Company A using a scale from "1" to "5" where "5" means "excellent" and "1" means "poor."

Respondent 1

	Poor				Excellent
	1	2	3	4	5
Overall satisfaction	○	○	○	○	●

Respondent 2

	Poor				Excellent
	1	2	3	4	5
Overall satisfaction	●	○	○	○	○

Q1a. IF "1" OR "5" IN Q1 ASK: Why did you give that rating?

Obtain respondent feedback in their own words

Another area where open-ended questions can be helpful is when you want to gather feedback on a brand, product, or service in the customers' own words. This can be especially powerful if you want to obtain their first, top-of-mind thoughts.

> Please tell us your perceptions of Product A. We are interested in your perceptions regardless of whether you've tried the product or not. Based on the product concept description above, what parts of the description are most appealing and why?

Analysis of open ends

Typically, open-ended responses are coded to provide an outcome of the percent of respondents that gave similar answers. This can be insightful and gives you a relative understanding of how many people feel the same way.

In the example below, customers that give Company A an excellent rating have stronger positive perceptions overall and particularly value their business hours and online banking service, positives that can be stressed in marketing materials. In contrast, those that rate Company A as poor have a more diffuse response with similar low scores across a wide range of responses. No one thing is causing dissatisfaction. As a result, the company might choose one or two things to work on in the near term and save the other items for later.

Rating of "5": Primary reason for rating Company A as excellent

Convenient hours	40%
Easy to use online banking	35%
Knowledgeable customer service ratings	15%
Good rates on checking accounts	5%
Other	5%

Rating of "1": Reasons for rating Company A as poor

Makes mistakes	12%
Inconvenient hours	9%
Bad customer service	8%
Too few branch locations	8%
Rates on CDs too low	7%
Doesn't have customer service reps available 24 hours a day	6%

Verbatim comments can also be pulled to help give context to the quantitative data and provide "customer flavor." As a rule of thumb, once all the open ends have been coded, the left over "other" responses should be no higher than 5 to 10 percent. If they are higher, it's a good idea to go back and recheck the coding to see if additional categories need to be added.

Chapter 13

Using Scales in Online Internet Research

There are many complexities in constructing useful scales for online research. It is important to understand the different types of scales and consider the subtle nuances of each type of scale. It is also important to evaluate any type of external factor that may be influencing the use of a specific type of scale.

Types of scales

There are three types of scales commonly used in market research: categorical, ordinal, and interval scales. Each scale is slightly different and each is used in different situations. Categorical scales refer to distinct measurements, such as yes or no. Ordinal scales generally refer to rankings. Interval scales refer to distinct number points on a scale and are typically used in performance ratings. Scale definitions and some examples of how they are used are provided below.

Categorical scales

Categorical scales, also referred to as nominal scales, assign codes to label items but they are not measurements. Some common examples of categorical scales are found in demographic questions where a code is assigned to label a group as in the examples below.

Are you male or female?

○ Male

○ Female

Please indicate your ethnicity.

○ 1 – Caucasian

○ 2 – African American

○ 3 – Asian

○ 4 – Native American

○ 5 – Other

Using the income categories below, please indicate the range that represents your total household income.

○ Less than $34,999

○ $35,000 – $49,999

○ $50,000 – $74,999

○ $75,000 or more

Ordinal scales

With an ordinal scale, numbers are assigned to items to represent order, such as rank order, but it does not provide any assessment of the space between the orders. For example, a survey may ask respondents to rank order their product preferences as in the question below.

From the list of soft drinks below, please rank your brand preference.

	Rank Order
Cola A	1
Cola B	5
Seltzer	4
Cola C	6
Soda A	3
Soda B	2

Determining rank using interval scales for performance or satisfaction sometimes does not provide much insight into ranking differentiation. For example, a respondent may provide the highest ranking equally for five attributes, but will not be able to differentiate which one is the best. A ranking question allows respondents to clearly differentiate the best from the worst.

What is not known from an ordinal scale is the space between rankings. From the example above, Cola A may be far ahead of other choices and Soda A and Soda B may be interchangeable substitutes in consumers' minds.

Interval scales

To circumvent the inability to measure the magnitude of the differences in points using an ordinal scale, surveys commonly use interval scales. Interval scales are used in importance ratings, customer satisfaction, agreement statements, and attribute ratings. Examples of questions that use interval scales are below.

Importance rating example

Below is a list of attributes that may or may not describe a laptop computer. For each attribute, please indicate the importance of each attribute using a scale from "0" to "10" where "0" is "not at all important" and "10" is "extremely important."

	Not at all Important									Extremely Important	
	0	1	2	3	4	5	6	7	8	9	10
Easy-to-use	O	O	O	O	O	O	O	O	O	O	O
Less than 5 lbs	O	O	O	O	O	O	O	O	O	O	O
Battery life 5+ hours	O	O	O	O	O	O	O	O	O	O	O
X gigs of memory	O	O	O	O	O	O	O	O	O	O	O

Customer satisfaction rating example

Please rate your experience at Company A using a scale from "0" to "10" where "0" is "very poor" and "10" is "excellent."

	Very poor										Excellent
	0	1	2	3	4	5	6	7	8	9	10
Ease of using online banking	O	O	O	O	O	O	O	O	O	O	O
Customer service rep's ability to resolve a problem	O	O	O	O	O	O	O	O	O	O	O
Interest rates on checking accounts	O	O	O	O	O	O	O	O	O	O	O

Agreement statements

Below is a list of statements about products/services from Company B. For each statement, please indicate how much you agree or disagree with the statement using the following scale:

1 = disagree strongly

2 = disagree somewhat

3 = neither agree nor disagree

4 = agree somewhat

5 = agree strongly

	1	2	3	4	5
Company B always has the books I'm looking for in stock	O	O	O	O	O
Company B hosts visiting authors frequently	O	O	O	O	O
Company B has a large music selection	O	O	O	O	O

Attribute ratings

Below is a list of product attributes for Product A. Please rate each attribute using a scale from "0" to "10" where "0" is "very poor" and "10" is "excellent."

	Very poor										Excellent
	0	1	2	3	4	5	6	7	8	9	10
Moisturizes skin for 24 hours	○	○	○	○	○	○	○	○	○	○	○
Has a sunscreen of SPF 15	○	○	○	○	○	○	○	○	○	○	○
Fresh scent	○	○	○	○	○	○	○	○	○	○	○

Interval scales allow for a variety of types of analysis including those related to averages and medians and those that measure variance in scales. They are especially useful in understanding differences in perceptions among different audiences and the magnitude of those differences. Top box and bottom box calculations are also quite common in the research industry. This involves summing the top two points (or bottom two points) on a scale.

Scale considerations

There are several questions to consider when deciding on which scale to use, including scale length, balanced and unbalanced scales, and visual display of the scale.

Balanced, unbalanced, and anchored scales

There is a classic debate within the market research community as to the actual layout of scales. Different researchers may often provide perfectly legitimate, but different answers. There are a few commonly used phrases associated with survey scales that must be understood before describing the different types of scales used today.

- **Balanced scales:** An equal number of answer selections that are positive as well as negative (e.g. extremely satisfied, somewhat satisfied, somewhat unsatisfied, very unsatisfied). Balanced scales provide the best sensitivity for both ends of a bipolar continuum.

- **Unbalanced scales:** An unequal number of answer selections that are positive versus negative. Generally, there are proportionately more positive answers than negative answers. If all the things being rated are at one end of the scale, then you lose discrimination if the scale is relatively short and does not have enough scale points at that end of the scale. This problem can be avoided with lots of scale points (e.g., rate "quality" on a scale from 1 to 100, where 100 means Excellent and 1 means Poor).

- **Anchored scales:** Use of a text identifier such as "extremely satisfied" at the end points of a scale. Scale imbalance can also occur with scales where only the end-points are anchored. This kind of imbalance may or may not be harmful to discrimination power, but it lacks the appearance of impartiality, and is probably not necessary.

Scale length

The following is a list of different types of scales used in customer satisfaction research, both balanced and unbalanced, and anchored and unanchored. In this set, categorical scales (for example, yes or no, single-punch or multi-punch questions) are not considered scale questions.

- 4-point scales; balanced and unbalanced.
- 5-point scales; balanced and unbalanced.
- 6-point or more scales; balanced and unbalanced.

Each scale has its pros and cons. Longer scales are better for analytical purposes (e.g., 9, 10, and 11) and will more effectively help monitor changes in business performance; it is easier to see when a downward or upward trend is beginning. The pitfall of larger scales is that each respondent might interpret a non-anchored data point differently. For example, one respondent might consider 7 a measure of satisfaction and another might consider it neutral. Shorter scales are easier for respondents, but provide less discrimination of the data. Regardless, if the sample selected for surveying is truly random and representative of the customer population, then differences in interpretation will level out. The following outlines the pros, cons, and suggested implementations of each specific type of scale.

4-point scales

The advantage of 4-point scales is that they are easy to administer, easy for respondents to understand, and easy for organizations to grasp. They are great for younger audiences as the respondents can easily discriminate among different points on the scale. In large organizations, employees can easily grasp the concept without any debate over the meaning. Shorter scales are commonly used with adults, but the drawback is that shorter scales minimize the ability to analyze variation in the data.

5-point scale with a neutral mid-point

A neutral mid-point means that respondents do not have to provide a positive or negative response. Typical mid-point statements include "neither satisfied nor dissatisfied" or "neutral."

A 5-point scale has many of the same benefits and drawbacks as a 4-point scale, but it does begin to allow some analysis of variance. Additionally, many researchers prefer to have midpoints in scales because many people in society are ambivalent to certain thoughts or ratings. Other researchers prefer to force respondents to provide a positive or negative response. The drawback of 5-point scales is that they still provide minimal adequate analysis of variance. Generally,

6-point or higher scales are needed to start to understand variance.

5-point scale without a neutral mid-point

Many researchers do not prefer to have a mid-point in their scales. This is called an unbalanced scale. Some researchers contend that respondents have a tendency to answer more positively to survey research—answers to normally distributed scales do not differentiate much. Therefore, these researchers believe it is important to provide more positive answers in the scales. An example of an unbalanced scale is:

- Extremely satisfied
- Very satisfied
- Somewhat satisfied
- Somewhat dissatisfied
- Extremely dissatisfied

In this unbalanced example, there are 3 positive answers and 2 negative answers. Scales with and without mid-points each have their advantages and disadvantages. Some researchers would contend that unbalanced scales such as the one above cannot effectively leverage standard statistical testing since those tests are based on normally distributed scales.

6-point or more scales

Scales that are 6 points or longer allow for improved analysis of variance. Statistically, they are much more effective at understanding differentiating opinions, but they generally add a bit more complexity for the respondents and the organization. Longer scales are quite commonly used. In fact, Frederich Reicheld, the inventor of the Net Promoter score, recommends an 11-point scale (0-10). Extending beyond 11 points on a scale is generally not advised. It does not provide any additional benefit to the analysis and also adds complexity into the research process.

Visual layout

Once you have decided on the scale range to use, it is important to consider scale layout. Determining the appropriate visual layout of scales has become increasingly important as companies begin developing web-based international research projects. Each country's reaction to the visual display of scales is influenced by their unique cultural behaviors and educational systems. Many factors can influence a respondent's understanding of the scale, including the distance between points on a scale, the number of points on a scale, and the direction in which the scale is displayed.

Unfortunately, a certain degree of non-sampling error exists in all surveys. However, the goal is to minimize that error. For web surveys, the visual layout of scales may impact how respondents answer specific questions and ultimately affect the aggregated results to those questions. Following these guidelines for the visual layout of scales in web surveys will help minimize non-sampling error and allow for the most reliable level of comparison possible for any given research study. Scale direction can be displayed in almost any fashion, but it is generally some methodological, cultural, technological, or historical factor that forces a specific implementation.

Scale direction considerations:

- Consistency in the direction of the scale
- Cultural influences
- Historical approaches
- Technology limitations

Scale consistency

Unfortunately, not all respondents read every detail of a survey, as researchers would like. This is why researchers should always keep surveys short, simple, and to the point. People get in the habit of responding to scales in a particular manner and may not pay attention to subtle changes in the direction of the scale, especially in longer surveys with multiple page breaks. Even if different scales of different length are being used, it is important that scales be consistently displayed in the same direction. It is not as important whether the scales are consistently displayed horizontally or vertically because there is an obvious delineation between vertical and horizontal scales. It is important to ensure consistent scale presentation across time and within a research study. Scales should always flow in a positive to negative direction or in a negative to positive direction. Never display scales in the opposite directions within the same survey. If the scale is consistently displayed in the same direction, then its direction does not matter because the non-sampling error is consistent across all questions and data sets.

Cultural influences

One of the most complicated issues when determining the direction of the scale is the impact that educational systems have on society's understanding of scales. These systems teach their students to think about scales in different ways. In North America and most of Europe, children are traditionally taught a quantitative orientation where 10 is good and 1 is bad on a 1 to 10 scale. This is the opposite in some countries where a rank-based orientation associates a 1 with good and a 10 with bad. This variation in interpretation of scales presents special considerations, especially if country-level information is being compared. In this situation, you must weigh the pros and cons of maintaining a consistent approach so that country-level information can be compared.

If the direction of the scale is flipped for various countries, then it is possible that more non-sampling error is introduced. If country comparison is less important and there is absolutely no future plan for scale comparison, then you may consider using different scale directions for different countries.

Historical approaches

Sometimes researchers are confronted with a choice between having inconsistent scale direction versus keeping historical trends. This is a difficult choice because on the one hand the data may have large amounts of non-sampling error and on the other, at least the data has been consistent wave over wave. In this case, it is best to evaluate each specific case individually.

Some of the factors that may be evaluated include:

- What proportion of the sample inverts the scale?
- How important to the business are the inverted questions? (e.g., are they compensation-based metrics? If so, then it might be best to leave them alone.)
- How will business colleagues react to a change in historical approaches?

When considering a change in scale, the first question to consider is whether the survey question was used in the past. If so, consider whether it is worth changing or not. If the new scale offers benefits that are superior to the old scale, then the new scale may be better for the organization. At this stage it is important to consider that there may be historical data quality trending concerns if the scale is changed.

This is usually a transition problem only. After a year or two with the new measurements, the organization usually has enough "new historic" data to satisfy its needs for historic comparison. Calibration or parallel testing (where the old and new scales are used in parallel for a while) is the best way to deal with this. However, it is also costly (essentially requiring doubling the sample sizes for a period of time), and many clients judge whether the improvements are worth the sacrifice and make a clean break if they are not. Generally, improving scale discrimination is not judged a sufficient reason to sacrifice historic comparisons, but sometimes measurement of a new dimension or in a significantly different way is.

Technology limitations

Sometimes there are technology limitations that prevent the use of certain types of scales and the layout of certain scales. Most web survey tools allow scales to be displayed in a horizontal or vertical fashion, but may be limited in more complicated grid questions where multiple questions share the same scale. For the most part, technology limitations are no longer a problem for survey research. Developers can generally create a solution to accommodate almost any type of scale. However, if technology is a barrier, secondary alternatives must be evaluated.

Intervals between points on a scale

Another important aspect to consider when designing web surveys is to ensure that the intervals between points on the scale are equidistant from each other. Unequal spacing can lead a respondent to think that differences intervals between the points should reflect how they feel about a certain attribute.

Many survey tools use a table-based framework in the background of an HTML page (such as Cascading Style Sheet, CSS) that sometimes affects how the scales are displayed on a website. Sometimes the size of the screen or the attributes in the left-most column will affect the spacing in the scale points. It is important that developers are explicitly directed to ensure that scale points are equidistant from each other.

Shading, colors, lines, visual cues, smiley faces

Introducing visual cues into a survey can have subtle unintended effects on a survey that can alter the data. It is extremely important that visual cues be thoroughly reviewed before they are implemented. It is generally advised not to use shades and colors in scales because whereas green can be positive in one culture, it could provoke a negative emotion in another country. Unless the study of the colors is the research issue, you should rarely use shades or colors in a multi-national study.

Visual cues may be acceptable in certain situations, but they must be used specifically for the audience being measured. For example, children may have difficulties understanding phrases or directions so visual cues will enable them to participate in a survey. Using smiley faces in an adult survey may elicit an unintended reaction among adults. Some adults may even be insulted by the use of certain imagery in a study and consider it childish or inappropriate.

Displaying values for each point

Another consideration for web surveys is whether to display numerical values for each scale point. Values do not need to be displayed for each scale point when:

1. Each point is associated with text (e.g., 5-point: Strongly Agree, Somewhat Agree, Agree, Somewhat Disagree, Strongly Disagree).

2. Displaying text anchors and the full range and equality of distance between scale points can be communicated visually (e.g., evenly spaced radio buttons).

Although it is not always necessary to display numerical values for each scale point, there are some advantages in doing so. Scale points with numerical values help respondents clearly identify the mid-point and each numerical location on a scale. This provides them with a better frame of reference when using these rating scales. It also reinforces the notion that each point on the rating scale is an equal distance from the previous and subsequent scale point.

If numerical values are used, each point on the scale should be labeled with its corresponding number. Labeling a subset of the scale points (e.g., odd numbers or anchors only) may create a response bias, in that respondents may be more likely to select the choices associated with a numerical value.

Displaying anchors and mid-points

A scale anchor is a word, phrase, or image that is placed near the two end points of a scale and generally describes what those end points mean. An anchor is typically used on a scale having seven or more points where the points between the two ends do not have any description associated with them. It is not necessary to anchor scales with seven or fewer points because they generally use text answers instead of numerical identifiers. In some cases a mid-point anchor may be used to describe neutrality or where the scale flips from positive to negative.

Scale anchors are almost always used in numeric scales that do not have a text descriptor at every point on the scale. They are useful because they signify what the extreme end points of a scale mean and they provide additional information about the objective of the question. Sometimes images are used instead of text responses. Images are especially useful in studies with children because they may not be able to interpret certain words or phrases.

Horizontal versus vertical orientation

Implementing a horizontal versus vertical orientation of the scale is dependent on a few factors, including the length of the scale and number of questions. Vertical scales are easier to implement with shorter scales that are four or five points long. Scales with eight or more points may pose difficulties in the visual appearance on a computer monitor, especially if the user has to scroll down to see the entire scale. Additionally, handling multiple questions in a vertical orientation can pose problems for displaying all of those questions in a succinct format.

In most online surveys, longer scales are displayed horizontally. For shorter scales, they are displayed both horizontally and vertically. There may be other business needs at play that influence the decision to display a scale horizontally or vertically such as legacy business issues.

Validation questions

As mentioned before, a certain amount of non-sampling error is to be expected in online surveys and scale questions pose difficult dilemmas because of cultural differences. Cultural influence on interpreting scales is an excellent example. No calculators exist to measure non-sampling errors, but questions can be written to estimate the non-sampling error due to the visual layout of the scale. In the example of the cultural miscoding, a follow-up confirmation question will suitably measure the impact.

For example, if a 0 to 10 scale is being used with 0 being a negative answer on the left side and 10 being a positive answer on the right side, one helpful exercise is to ask respondents to confirm whether they are in fact satisfied (or dissatisfied). The confirmation question will be displayed based on branching rules from the first question. If a respondent selects points 7 through 10, the confirmation question may say, "Were you in fact satisfied?" and follow with answers, "Yes, I was satisfied" and "No, I was not satisfied."

The confirmation question will provide a good assessment of how much of the sample is impacted by a specific type of non-sampling error. However, it does not tell you why the respondents misinterpreted the question, or if they did at all. Additional follow-up questions will need to be added to further investigate the data.

Another related issue is to determine how to treat the data that is misinterpreted. It is not sound to change the data because respondents' true meanings of the survey responses have been captured. Even if a "why" question is asked, there may be a certain amount of non-sampling error in the "why" that prevents a researcher from changing a respondent's answer. If any data are going to be altered, it is best to set predefined screening rules that are consistently applied across the entire dataset. This will prevent any subjective or biased analysis and interpretation of the data.

Finding the preferred approach

The preferred approach ultimately depends on specific client objectives and the geographies in which the survey is being conducted. It is important to take into account the factors being considered above as well as specific client objectives. A thoughtful discussion with the team will be required to determine a preferred approach.

Chapter 14

Use of Multimedia in Online Research

Online research has an advantage over other methodologies in that it allows marketers to gather feedback on visual content, both static pictures and streaming video, typically at lower costs than alternative methodologies such as in-person interviews or focus groups. In addition, the growth of high speed Internet access means more people can view visual content in a survey without the frustration of slow downloading times that could lead to higher incomplete rates. Online surveys also allow for the volume of response needed to make statistical projections to a target audience, a benefit that is generally too costly to do with other methodologies.

Online surveys can be used to evaluate visual content for a variety of business needs such as:

- Advertising testing
- Package design
- Logo recognition
- Programming content evaluation
- Measurement of brand variants
- Product placement/retail display
- Concept testing

Essentially, anywhere a picture can be used as a visual prompt can be incorporated into an online survey and evaluated.

Risks and concerns

There are several important risks and concerns to consider when incorporating images or video into an online survey.

Security

First, while there are many security features that can be used to safeguard highly sensitive company material, there is nothing that is one hundred percent effective. There is nothing that can prevent respondents from taking a picture or video of what they see on screen and distributing it more broadly. That said, security breaches do not happen often and are typically associated with companies or products that get a lot of buzz. Security is something to keep in mind particularly with new concept or advertising testing and balanced against the cost savings from an online methodology versus the impact of a potential security breach.

For static images, pictures can be encrypted so respondents cannot use a snag function or program to capture the picture. To add another layer of security, the picture can be broken into pieces, much like a puzzle, and each piece encoded. Video can be secured by allowing respondents to view the video only once and then have the video disabled. Another alternative is to have respondents click on a link within the survey that serves up the video only once per respondent identification code.

Image/video formats

There are a variety of different methods to display images and videos in an online survey. File formats most commonly used are ones that have the lightest footprint (small memory size) or are commonly used today on the Internet. Specific tools are able to handle specific file formats. For example, Windows Media Player does not play an Apple file. Image and video formats can be resource-intense and require the assistance of an IT professional. Most survey tools can handle basic technology.

The most common formats used for images include:

- Joint Photographic Experts Group (.jpg)
- Tagged Image File (.tif)
- Graphical Interchangeable Format file (.gif)
- Photoshop document (.psd)
- Bitmap image file (.bmp)

The most common formats used for videos include:

- Moving Picture Experts Group (.mp4 and .mpg)
- Apple QuickTime Movie (.mov)
- Flash video (.swf)
- Windows media file (.wmv)
- Real media file (.rm)

Video file formats are generally proprietary and can only be used by the manufacturer's tool. For example, a .mov file cannot be played inside of Windows Media Player. It is best played inside of Apple's QuickTime. For videos, most people have QuickTime and Windows Media Player installed on their computers. If not, the tools can easily be prompted for installation.

Download times

Download times vary depending on the size of the image/video file and the respondent's modem speed. It is important to take download time into consideration when estimating survey length. It can be aggravating for respondents if they agree to a 20-minute survey and then have the image download time add ten minutes. This could lead to higher incompletion rates. The good news is that more and more people have broadband connections, so download times are less problematic. In addition, surveys can be programmed so that the visual content is downloaded in the background while the respondent is answering other questions. This has the obvious benefit of saving time.

Implementing applications into research

Web-based studies offer researchers a wide variety of tools to improve research capabilities. These improvements lead to more effective implementations of the research. The following are a few situations in which technology enables more effective online research.

Advertising testing

Respondents can be shown storyboards, rough cut ads, or fully finished ads depending on the business issue. If an advertising or PR group within your organization has completed the boards and stored them on a digital format, then the research tool should be able to easily implement them.

Concept testing

To determine which advertising concept is the best alternative to take to full production, respondents can be shown a series of still shots, usually six to ten images, with commentary on the ad provided either as captions beneath the pictures or as an audio overlay. Respondents are asked basic questions to rate the appeal of the ad, their interest in the product or service as a result of the ad, and likelihood to purchase. Respondents can also be asked to rank order the concepts.

Tracking

Once an ad has aired on television, it can be tracked to assess how it is performing in market. Respondents are shown either a series of stills that represent the ad or the ad itself and asked whether they recall seeing the ad and its impact on likelihood to purchase. Most companies use a series of stills pulled from the finished ad with the brand name of the product or service masked to assess whether respondents link the advertising with the brand.

Package design

Online surveys can be used to evaluate package design. Respondents can be shown variations of package designs and asked to rank order their preferences. Images or videos must be stored in a digital format. The digital format can be inserted into the research tool.

Programming content evaluation

Respondents can evaluate short programming content, such as news clips or show segments. They are first shown a video of the content and then asked a series of questions about various elements of the program. This methodology does not work well for content longer than a few minutes. After the video is shown, the respondent will then be asked questions about that video content. Lengthy videos lead to lengthy studies. Lengthy studies lead to survey attrition. Naturally, this can be counteracted with survey incentives, but this drives up study costs.

Measurement of brand variants

The ability to show the specific packaging in an online survey ensures the correct brand variant gets credit on measures such as awareness, usage, and purchase behavior.

Product placement/retail display

Respondents can also be prompted with an image to measure awareness of a special retail promotion or store display.

Chapter 15

Online Qualitative Tools

Online qualitative tools are typically used to explore various topics with the target audience. The most common online tools are message boards, focus groups, one-on-one interviews, and video diaries. All four of the research methods use similar tools, but they differ based on scheduling and the number of participants. The attractive feature of these tools is that since they are online, participants can respond from any computer that can access the Internet.

The actual methodologies for online message boards, online focus groups, one-on-one interviews, and video diaries are quite different. An online message board generally occurs over a period of time (two or three days), whereas an online focus group generally occurs at a specific point in time. Online focus groups tend to be two hours long just like a traditional focus group. A one-on-one interview is scheduled for a specific length of time and includes only the moderator and participant. Generally, a one-on-one interview is best accompanied with audio (over a telephone or the Internet). Video diaries take place over a specified length of time and are excellent for testing a series of products over time.

Advantages and disadvantages

The advantage of these forums is that they are especially useful for audiences that are more technical and distributed across multiple geographic locations. IT pros or heavy Internet users may be more inclined to participate in an online message board since they can participate during a time that is comfortable for them. Additionally, an Internet-based dialogue suits personalities that are more introverted. They typically feel more comfortable collaborating in a discussion on the Internet.

The primary disadvantage is that online qualitative tools can sometimes cost more. Online focus groups and online message boards generally have more participants than a traditional focus group. An online message group will have up to 30 participants. Incentives for 30 participants will cost more, compared with the costs for a traditional focus group of eight to twelve. Additionally, moderating a message board over a three-day period requires more time than a traditional two-hour focus group would. Researchers charge based on hours spent. Between incentive costs and research hours, online message boards can become quite expensive.

Using forums

There are many great uses for online qualitative tools. They are excellent for testing concepts since imagery and graphics can be displayed within the board. Actual product concepts can be compared and respondents can interact virtually similar to a traditional qualitative setting. This model easily extends into advertisement and website testing. Online qualitative tools can show video or graphics, so advertisements are easily reviewed in this portal. Various websites can easily be tested directly within the tool.

Online qualitative tools are also good for discussing sensitive or emotional topics. If respondents are reluctant to discuss topics that elicit strong emotions, sitting behind a computer in the privacy of their own home may generate good conversations. Without the possibility of being identified, online respondents feel freer to discuss private aspects of their lives.

Important functions of online qualitative tools

Basic functions of online qualitative tools must include a moderator view and a respondent view. A helpful function is a mechanism to allow the sponsoring company the ability to observe the boards without having the ability to influence the boards directly.

There are important features that must be addressed depending on the type of research being conducted. For example, a product concept test reviewing a set of images requires the tool to have the functionality to support the images within the tool. Hosting images is fairly easy for online tools. Other more complicated features include videos, audio communication through the tool itself, and webcam capabilities. Webcams are still not commonly used because many end users do not have them. Bandwidth availability is also an issue with webcams. Disruptions in focus groups that use webcam technology are quite common.

The "Observer" view: a patent dispute

iTracks purchased a patent from Greenfield Online that purportedly grants it full licensing over the "Observer" or "Client" view. It has not been regularly enforced as nearly all qualitative online solutions have some form of a client view enabled. However, as iTracks continues to push this patent, it may have implications on the capabilities of the tools in the future. Vendors have built alternative options that allow observers to watch the board while it is going on.

Costs to conduct online message boards

Many vendors will provide the tool itself to conduct the online qualitative study. There is a plethora of vendors who conduct this type of research, but they either lease the software from another company or use proprietary software. To save a large amount of money, it is possible to lease the software independently of a research company, but it is a significant research undertaking. Leasing the software is similar to using an online survey vendor. However, this is a different type of research.

Depending on the type of audience being researched, a fully serviced three-day board will likely cost anywhere between $15,000 and $35,000. The large difference in costs is due to incentives and professional fees. Typical incentives range from $50 to $250 per participant, depending on the type of respondent being recruited. Taking the most extreme case, an incentive of about $250 each for 30 respondents adds up $7,500. Adding service and delivery fees, vendors are likely to mark these costs up to $10,000. Professional fees for three continuous days of project management add an extra few thousand dollars. Software leasing fees, study design, and reporting quickly get the costs up. Of course, vendors must make a profit too. With the exception of incentives and software leasing fees, much of the costs can be mitigated. Conducting the study without the help of a full-service research firm will bring the costs down significantly. At a minimum, there will be two out-of-pocket charges—the software licensing fees and respondent incentives.

Costs to conduct online focus groups

Online focus groups may cost the same or less than traditional focus groups. All functions of online and offline focus groups proceed similarly including study design, study implementation, reporting, and paying incentives. A traditional, offline focus group incurs costs that an online group will not. These costs generally include facility fees, travel costs for the moderator, and any expenses to provide refreshments for the participants. Study design, participant recruitment, and reporting should be consistent across both types of studies.

Video diaries and one-on-one interviews

The costs for video diaries and one-on-one interviews can vary quite a bit, depending on the vendor. Since ads or concepts are typically tested in these methodologies, the type of technology enabled in the research platforms can have a significant impact on costs. For example, if video features are enabled for respondents to view, one tool may offer this ability; another may not. This should have an impact on costs. Additionally, if products need to be shipped to the homes or businesses of the participants, this adds costs.

Tools vendors

There are a few vendors that lease their software for online message boards. All of these tools offer similar features including image hosting, videos, interactive discussions, moderator views, client views, and participant views. A list of tool providers appears in the Appendix. This may not be a complete list, but it does provide a solid overview of some of the more widely-used or high-quality products available on the market.

Chapter 16

Privacy and Security

There are many facets of security that are important for the respondent, the survey company, and the sponsoring business. For the respondent, the most important feature of research software is to ensure confidentiality and privacy. For the survey companies, the software must be impenetrable, the respondents' privacy must be ensured, high-quality data must be ensured, and content should be secure. For the sponsoring business, respondents' privacy must be ensured and the content must remain confidential. There are overlapping priorities for each interested party. Keep in mind that none of the solutions are completely impenetrable, but some of the security measures are more effective than others.

CASRO has an excellent Code of Standards document which can be accessed at *www.casro.org/codeofstandards.cfm*. If there are specific questions about the ramifications of security or privacy breaches, this comprehensive document should provide excellent guidance.

Respondent security

An important measure for nearly all respondents is privacy and confidentiality. In the survey process, it is not uncommon for contact information of the respondents to be readily available or for the respondents to provide their contact information. Despite having this available, it may not be appropriate for the company conducting the research to release this information beyond the actual data collection. There are a few different methods that can be implemented to prevent the release of information to the sponsoring business.

Research tools allow the ability to view contact information with a simple on/off–type switch. If you wish to see contact information (and the respondent provides it), you can simply select a feature that enables you to view the Personally Identifiable Information. This setting can be modified at any point in the research process. If confidentiality is important, then prudence is the best option. Prevent the information from becoming available.

In many surveys, researchers ask for the contact information in a question at the end of the survey. If prudence is required, eliminating this question is a good idea. If the question is asked, the information can be hidden in the resulting data file.

Executives often want to see contact information, especially in employee-satisfaction research. They sometimes feel that they need to know the information in order to fix any difficult situation in the company. It is a good idea to steer executives away from this idea.

Company security

Many of the security features required by CASRO and ESOMAR must be enabled within the online research tool. The survey tool should be the primary guard against research security threats. The research tool must be accountable for:

- General guidelines to prevent respondents from gaming the survey
- Keeping product and ad concepts confidential
- Ensuring high-quality data with unique survey links

Preventing respondents from gaming the survey

A common approach used by panel companies is to provide monetary-based incentives to complete a survey. This can sometimes encourage respondents to cheat the survey process. As these types of respondents become more familiar with the survey process, they begin to understand how to take a survey so that they can qualify to participate. Preventing respondents who cheat the survey process is critical to ensuring high-quality data. There are a few methods that can be leveraged to mitigate the effect of cheaters.

Ensure that each link sent to an email address is unique. One link distributed to a mass of respondents provides each individual the opportunity to complete the survey more than once. This decreases the quality of the data set and it will be apparent in the aggregated results.

A method more commonly used today is to insert a cookie on each respondent's computer. This enables the online tool to recognize that the same person is taking the survey multiple times. If a cookie is identified on a respondent's computer, the link can be automatically disabled. It is possible for respondent's to prevent cookies from being put on their computers and they can also delete their cookie history. This technology does not prevent all respondents from cheating the survey process, but it is one step to help minimize cheating respondents.

Passwords are also an option for online research. This is not commonly used for quantitative studies as it puts an undue burden on the respondent and is not necessary if the survey link is unique. However, for qualitative studies in which multiple participants attend a group event, passwords should be required.

Protecting confidentiality

Protecting survey content in an online study is extremely difficult. There are survey systems that make it more difficult to copy the content, but respondents can merely capture a screen shot of their desktops if they want to save the image. Even videos can be copied with specialized software that records the information being displayed on a screen. Depending on the sensitivity of the information, it may be better to conduct a study via telephone or in person. Even if your respondents did not capture the image, there is little that can be done to prevent them from posting the information on a blog.

SurveyClip (*www.surveyclip.com*) is a company that specializes in keeping content secure for online studies. Specifically, its goal is to keep audio and video content from being copied. If cheaters are unable to break its application in the future, this could have fantastic benefits for new product and advertisement testing. Instead of posting a question or paragraph in a survey, which can easily be copied, the product and advertising content can be played in the audio or video file. Questions that follow the content in the survey will not need to outline the product or advertisement concept; they merely need to reference the original audio or video file. Although companies like Surveyclip are making great progress in keeping content secure, caution must be given to avoid simple hacks such as video recording the information being displayed on a computer.

Ensuring high-quality data with unique survey links

In the first few years of online research, survey vendors would post one survey link that all respondents could access. Today, advanced survey tools assign unique links that are sent individually to each email address. This should be a basic requirement of all online research tool vendors. Avoid vendors who are unable to provide this basic level of functionality. It is important to keep the survey link unique as this prevents the survey from being completed more than once. Access to the study can also be controlled.

Each link should be protected by using an https assignment. Although not completely necessary this does ensure the link is kept secure. Additionally, the unique links should assign random letters and numbers to each survey. It is extremely important that numbering or lettering not follow a sequential order. Control over the survey links prevents respondents from attempting to take the survey multiple times.

Chapter 17

Research with Children

Conducting research with children presents its own set of difficulties beyond tailoring the content for a child to understand. Most importantly, most countries require parental consent before surveying children. This requires some extra steps in the research process that are undoubtedly going to impact study costs.

Every country is different regarding the requirements to conduct research with children. In the U.S., CASRO has outlined that anyone under 18 must have parental consent (http://www.casro.org/codeofstandards.cfm). In the UK, the Market Research Society (MRS) has produced a similar document outlining requirements to research children. This organization defines children as anyone under age 16.

MRS has specifically outlined the requirements for surveying children in section B.26: Consent of a parent or responsible adult (acting *in loco parentis*) must be obtained before interviewing a child under age 16 in the following circumstances:

- In home/at home (face-to-face and telephone interviewing)
- Group discussions/depth interviews
- Postal questionnaires
- Internet questionnaires
- Email
- Where interviewer and child are alone together
- In public places such as in-street/in-store central locations

Directory of Online Survey Research Tools

This book does not attempt to evaluate all of the survey tools available, but it does provide a list of the more commonly used survey tools and some other resources to identify tools to use. There are hundreds of survey tools available and a search online will quickly identify many of them. Useful search terms include "online survey tool," "online research survey," or "internet survey tool." Two other research organizations have a decent list of the tools available today and are available at:

- *http://www.mrdc.co.uk/links.php*
- *http://www.quirks.com/software/web_results.asp*

Introductory survey tools

For those who want access to a basic survey tool without spending a lot of money, two companies fit the bill. You may also want to look into companies that are described in the mid-tier section, as many of them offer entry-level packages at a reasonable price.

SurveyMonkey (www.surveymonkey.com)

SurveyMonkey is a web-based tool that supports over 15 types of questions including single and multiple response, open-ends, scales, grid questions with single- and multiple-response answers, grid questions with multiple scales, numeric text boxes, and the ability to upload images. You can also randomize answers, require questions, and add skip logic. SurveyMonkey has survey templates you can access and the tool supports any language. You can try the basic package for free.

The tool has a variety of customizable themes you can choose from to tailor the look and feel of your survey. Invitations can be sent by email or by including a link on your website. You also have the ability to create pop-up invitations on your website.

Like most survey tools, you can monitor the progress of your survey in real time and download results in Excel, .csv, or PDF formats. SurveyMonkey also offers the ability to create crosstabs and filters. You can also create charts and graphs.

The company offers three tiers of service. The basic package is available for free, though you are limited to just ten questions per survey and only 100 responses per survey. This is a great way to try out the software. It can also come in handy for quick projects or incidence checks. SurveyMonkey Pro is the middle-tier offering and for less than $20 per month, the surveys can include an unlimited number of questions with up to 1,000 responses. If you run over the 1,000 completes in a month, you are charged a small response fee. The Unlimited Annual Package is the most popular option and allows for unlimited questions and unlimited responses, all for a few hundred dollars a year.

Zoomerang.com (www.zoomerang.com)

Zoomerang is a web-based application that provides 15 different types of questions including single response, rating scale, open-ends, and access to a survey template library. You can include skip and brand logic, upload images, and randomize answer choices. Currently, it does not have the ability to handle a grid question with multiple responses. You can also access its panel for samples.

For analysis, Zoomerang offers statistical analysis and tag clouds, a feature that lets you tag frequently used phrases and an online sample size calculator. You are also able to create customized charts and results can be downloaded to an Excel, PowerPoint, or PDF file.

Surveys can be deployed via a personalized email and by posting a web link. You can also deploy the survey to mobile phones.

Zoomerang offers three levels of service—basic, Pro, and Premium packages. It offers the basic package for free as a trial, which allows you to ask 30 questions and gather 100 completes. With both the Pro and Premium packages, you can ask an unlimited amount of questions and gather an unlimited amount of completes. The tool functionality increases with each package tier. Zoomerang supports 40 languages and results can be monitored in real time.

Mid-tier survey tools

There are many mid-tier survey tools available that offer more robust functionality at all stages of the research process, from survey creation, to deployment, to results analysis.

Apian Software (www.apian.com)

Apian Software offers two types of engagement. You can send them your questionnaire and it will handle the rest or you can access the survey tool directly. It also offers a 30-day free trial download of the survey tool. Apian is one of the few companies that can handle multimedia methodologies by allowing you to distribute the survey via the web, paper, local area network, or kiosk. The data can then be combined for holistic analysis.

Its questionnaire functionality includes 32 pre-defined scales as well as the ability to customize scales. The tool has check box questions as well as grid questions with single or multiple columns that can handle scales and write in answers. You can also upload images. Functionality includes the ability to require questions, randomize questions within a grid, randomize answers, pause/resume survey, and skip logic from both single- and multiple-answer questions. The tool also supports piping from both prior questions within the survey as well as passing data based on a respondent password or ID.

Apian's SurveyPro supports multiple languages. You have the ability to customize fonts, screen colors, add graphics and your logo to match your website, or to quickly apply a screen look pulled from a set of templates. The tool has instant online reporting so you can watch field progress.

The survey tool allows you to send email invitations, reminders, and thank you messages. Data can be exported to SQL, MS Access, and .csv, and the cross-tab function can accommodate up to 500 banner points. Data can be displayed in a table or as a graphic display.

SurveyPro is offered as a web-based application, a monthly subscription, or a full licensing option that allows you to run the software on your own servers. The subscription option sells for about $100 each month. The survey software is offered for free, but you pay for file storage space. The subscription option does not require a contract and allows you one active survey per file and up to 2,000 questions and 50,000 completes per month. The full license version allows for unlimited surveys, an unlimited number of questions per survey, and unlimited responses. The software allows you to deploy surveys from your own server and costs range from just under $1,000 to about $2,000 per user.

Constant Contact (www.constantcontact.com)

Constant Contact provides email marketing, online marketing event support, and an online survey tool. It also offers a free 60-day trial. Constant Contact has over sixty survey templates available and uses simple drag and drop functionality to modify surveys. Constant Contact is not a market research company so its online survey functionality is limited. It supports seven different types of sample survey questions such as single answer, multiple answers, rating scales, and open-ended questions. Constant Contact does not offer grid questions or numeric text questions. You can customize the look and feel of your survey by changing colors and fonts and adding images.

You can invite respondents to your survey either by sending them an email invitation or posting a URL link to the survey on your website. Constant Contact enables you to export results in .csv format and filter responses.

Constant Contact is a web-based application that offers only one simple, straightforward pricing option for its online survey tool. You pay less than $20 per month, which allows for up to 5,000 survey responses. If you run over 5,000 survey responses, you pay a small fee per responses over the 5,000. The package also includes an unlimited polling function, free of charge that allows you to create polls on your website. The software can handle up to ten polls running simultaneously.

Grapevine Surveys (www.grapevinesurveys.com)

Grapevine's online survey tool is similar to other online survey tools in that you can create the survey, collect responses, and analyze results. You can create a survey from scratch or choose a starting point from its library of over 240 templates. Grapevine offers tiered products to fit a range of budgets. However, unlike other survey companies, Grapevine does not vary the survey functionality by product tier. The full set of features and functionality is available to everyone regardless of the product package they buy. Instead, Grapevine creates its product packages based on the number of interviews to be conducted within a specific period.

Grapevine has the full range of question types you are likely to need, including drop-down boxes, grid questions that allow for single and multiple responses per row, rating scales, and text boxes. In addition, the survey tool offers the ability to add an "Other," "NA," or "none of the above" to response sets as well as the ability to require a question, randomize the answer order, and upload images into questions. You can also incorporate skip logic as well as less common offerings such as branching and skip logic with multiple answers and piping. The tool can also support multiple languages.

In addition, Grapevine allows you to export results to Excel, SPSS, and create a PDF. The tool has crosstab and filter capabilities for analysis.

Grapevine is a web-based survey software solution with three account options, plus a free trial. The 30 day free trial package allows you to test drive the survey tool with up to 25 responses. They also offer a per survey package for single users called the Quick Account that is good for 90 days and allows for up to 1,000 responses. The cost for this option is just under $500 per survey. A Basic Account is a single user annual account that lets you conduct an unlimited number of surveys and collect up to 3,000 responses. This package is about $1,000 and additional users can be added for $500 per user. Its Premium Account runs about $3,500 per year and offers unlimited surveys and up to 10,000 responses. Additional responses cost $0.25 per response. An unlimited number of users can access the survey tool with this package.

Hosted Surveys (www.hostedsurvey.com)

Hosted Surveys offers a do-it-yourself survey tool as well as the ability to outsource the entire project to Hosted Surveys to manage. The do-it-yourself survey tool allows you to create a survey from scratch, modify existing surveys, and combine survey questions from different templates from their library. The survey tool has the standard types of questions including multiple choice—select all that apply, multiple choice—single answer, drop-down boxes, grid or matrix questions that use a single scale or double scale, and of course open-ended text boxes. You are also able to randomly rotate question answers and required questions.

The survey tool allows you to monitor results in real time and download data into Microsoft Excel, Access, or XML. You are able to modify the look and feel of the survey by specifying the font, color, style, and background of the text. You can also include a logo and upload images to a page. Similar to other online survey software, Hosted Surveys offers the ability to create your own personalized email invitations and pop-up invitations on your site. The pop up invites can be programmed to appear with every visitor, randomly, or at set intervals.

Hosted Surveys is a web-based survey application that offers response-level packages and two private label options. Its response packages offer a cost per response ranging from $25 for 50 responses up to $4,000 for 20,000 responses. The response allotment can be spread over an unlimited number of surveys and the packages are good for 18 months after the date of purchase. Hosted Surveys' private label option is offered as either a web-based solution or as a full license package. Pricing for the web-based solution is a combination of designer and administrative fees for creating and maintaining the look and feel of the software. Designer/administrative fees can run up to roughly $5,000 annually and response charges can range from a couple of thousand annually to several tens of thousands of dollars annually depending on the response package purchased. Hosted Surveys also has a private label, in-house version that allows you to host and manage surveys on your own servers. Charges include a one-time license fee that varies depending on the number of expected end users and an annual maintenance fee. Costs to get you started with this plan range from several thousand dollars up to several tens of thousands of dollars depending on the number of users.

InfoPoll (www.infopoll.com)

InfoPoll offers a free, Windows-based program to create surveys. The company charges for survey hosting, done on its servers and server packages so you can host on your own servers. The survey tool supports a variety of question types including multiple-choice questions, single-response questions, rating scales, grid questions with single and multiple responses, grid questions with multiple scales, open-ended questions, and numeric text boxes. Like other survey tools, InfoPoll allows you to program, preview, and test your survey before launch. InfoPoll offers the ability to monitor survey results in real time and create customized reports, crosstabs, and the ability to download survey data to other applications like Excel.

The company offers free testing and a trial and a short, 30-day project can run under $50. Small scale surveys with fewer than 400 respondents and 30 days of hosting ranges from about $50 up to about $200. If the survey runs longer than 30 days, you pay $50 for each additional 30 days. Standard projects of 400 to 10,000 respondents run about $500 for 30 days of hosting. If you need to run longer than that, InfoPoll charges a hundred dollars for each additional 30 days of hosting. You can also pay a minimal fee of $50 per month for data storage. InfoPoll can also accommodate very large-scale studies of over 10,000 respondents. The company charges about $500 for the first 10,0000 respondents and $400 for each additional block of 10,000 respondents. The same charges apply for extended field time and data storage. InfoPoll also offers flexible software licensing agreements. Call for details.

Inquisite (www.inquisite.com)

In July 2009, Inquisite was acquired by Allegiance, Inc., a company that offers customer and employee loyalty and engagement management software. Inquisite's software can be either hosted or installed onsite. It offers two products, Inquisite Survey and Inquisite EPM, its Employee Performance Management system.

Inquisite Survey is the general survey tool for standard research projects ranging from concept testing to brand awareness measurement to customer satisfaction. It can support table or grid questions, multi-scale grid questions, open-ended questions, embedded images and links as well as skip logic, piping, and branching. The company offers a free 30-day trial as well as a live demo.

Inquisite offers three optional modules for its survey tool. The Multi-Language kit allows you to translate your survey into multiple languages and set specific parameters by language, such as multi-byte character languages used in Asia. The Software Development Kit allows you to further customize your surveys. The Respondent Management Module allows you to import and manipulate your internal databases to create your own in-house custom panels.

Inquisite Survey has an invitation wizard to create and schedule email invites and the ability to import data in a .csv file. Like other online survey tools, you can also create pop-up invitations. Inquisite software also allows you to create a random sample or a panel sample. You can create customized charts, crosstabs, filters, and download the data into .csv, MDB, and SPSS formats.

Inquisite Survey has both a web-based application and a license agreement option, but pricing is not available on its website. You must contact the company for specifics.

InstantSurvey (http://www.instantsurvey.com)

InstantSurvey provides two versions of its online survey tool. Instant-Survey Basic and InstantSurvey Pro offer the same functionality in terms of questionnaire design. InstantSurvey Pro includes additional functionality on the backend with the ability to create reports, cross-tab statistical analytics, and access to its chart wizard function. Both versions allow you to import word documents and turn them into a questionnaire or access questionnaire templates. The question types included are single response, grid questions with single response, rating scales, multiple-response questions, open-ended questions, numeric text boxes, and the ability to upload images. Both versions allow for required questions, piping, and skip logic. However, only the InstantSurvey Pro can handle randomized questions. Both surveys can accommodate 20 different languages and let you customize the look and feel of the survey, or choose a graphic template.

You can deploy your surveys by creating an email invite, upload-ing your email list to distribute through the InstantSurvey site, or mailing out from your company's email system. The survey tool also enables you to post a link to the survey on your website or create pop-up invitations.

If you need to acquire a sample, InstantSurvey has a partnership with Global Test Market, a global online panel company. Similar to other survey companies, InstantSurvey lets you view results in real time and graph questionnaire responses. The program also gives you the ability to look at respondent level data.

InstantSurvey is a web application and offers a free trial of Instant-

Survey Basic. The company uses a response volume-pricing plan. The Basic version will cost from less than $30 a month for up to 200 responses to just under $70 for 1,000 responses per month. You can also purchase one of the response level Basic packages on an annual basis for a discount. The Pro version has additional functionality as mentioned, and for less than $100 a month you can collect up to 500 responses. At the high end, you can purchase up to 10,000 completes a month for a few hundred dollars. The Pro version is also sold as an annual package for a discount. With both the Basic and Pro versions of the survey tool, if you run over your response allotment you will be charged an additional $0.25 per complete.

KeySurvey.com (www.keysurvey.com)

KeySurvey is an online survey tool that includes 15 different customizable question types including single-response questions, multiple-response questions, matrix questions, rating scales, open-ends, and numeric text boxes. KeySurvey also offers a questionnaire library. The survey tool supports skip logic, question and answer randomization, branching, piping, and required questions. The survey tool can also accommodate surveys in any language. You can customize the look and feel of your survey by changing the background colors, fonts, and adding a logo. You can also use KeySurvey's pre-defined color palette or access its theme library.

The survey tool allows you to send out invitations via email, post a link on your website, or create pop-ups. You can also personalize the look and feel of your invite. In terms of analysis, the survey tool has crosstab and data filtering capabilities as well as significance testing. You can also create customized charts and export data in PDF, Excel, .csv, and SPSS formats.

KeySurvey offers a 30-day free trial of its survey tool and a 60-day evaluation period for its Enterprise solution. You can also take a visual tour or schedule a product demonstration. The company offers three packages. The Professional package provides unlimited surveys, unlimited questions, and unlimited responses for one user for about

$6,000 per year. The Workgroup package also has unlimited surveys, questions, and responses, in addition to accommodating multiple users. This package runs about $9,000 for a year. There is also an Enterprise package that can accommodate any number of users and can be integrated with other systems applications such as a CRM system. Pricing for this option is available upon request.

Qualtrics (www.qualtrics.com)

Qualtrics offers the Qualtrics Research Suite to both academic and corporate organizations. You can sign up for a free trial or to watch a free demo. You also have access to a question library. Similar to other online survey tools, Qualtrics supports multiple-choice questions with single and multiple responses, matrix or grid questions, scale questions, rank ordering, open-ended questions, drop-down boxes, and numeric text boxes. However, Qualtrics also offers hot spots and heat map functionality. The survey tool supports skip logic, branching, piping, multiple languages, randomization of answers, and answer blocks. In addition, you can post graphics as well as videos and sound clips.

Qualtrics Research Suite allows you to create crosstabs, filters, and customizable reports. You can also run statistics such as mean and standard deviation and export data into Excel, SPSS, XML, and HTML.

Qualtrics provides the ability to send email invites from its servers or from your company's servers. The survey tool includes functionality to review the mail history of a survey and generate random samples from your internal databases. You can also send reminder messages and review respondent survey history.

The company offers a professional license for $5,000 annually that allows for up to 10,000 completes and includes training and support. You can try out the software on a per study basis that will cost you about $500 for the software and $1 to $2 per complete. The company does not have pricing information on its website. Instead, you need to fill out a contact form and a representative will contact you to talk through your needs and determine the best package to meet them.

QuestionPro (www.questionpro.com)

QuestionPro offers three tiers of service—a free basic package, a professional level package, and the corporate package. Most of the basic survey functionality is available in all packages, though the corporate package offers access to higher-level features and functionality. The corporate package allows for more sophisticated questionnaire programming, multi-language studies, access to the questionnaire template library, and the ability to manage a volume of surveys. In addition, the corporate package has more capabilities on the backend such as the ability to export data to MS PowerPoint and create time series and segmentation analysis.

All versions of the survey tool support a variety of question types including multiple choice–single response, multiple choice–multiple response, ratings scales, open-ended responses, numeric text boxes, and the ability to require questions. Only the corporate package allows for randomized questions, answers, piping, and skip logic. In addition, this is one of the few packages that can handle video as well as still images.

You can view survey results in real time and data can be exported to Excel, SPSS, or as a raw data .csv file. With QuestionPro, you can deploy your survey via email, a link posted on your website, or a pop-up on your website. Pop-ups can also be programmed to appear to every *n*th visitor and new site visitors. QuestionPro accommodates customized graphics and offers a free trial of the basic package.

The free trial allows for one survey of up to ten questions and an unlimited number of responses. The mid-level package, called Web Professional, is less than $20 per month and includes unlimited surveys, an unlimited number of questions and unlimited responses. This package also includes access to QuestionPro's survey library, the ability to copy surveys and questions, and to create a personal survey library. The Corporate package costs about $100 per month for unlimited surveys, unlimited questions, and unlimited responses. This option also includes all the functionality of the Web Professional version plus more sophisticated survey features such as question and answer randomization, text piping, and complex branching logic. You can also have your respondents upload files, such as bills, that can be used as verification or for additional analysis.

SnapSurveys (www.snapsurveys.com)

SnapSurveys provides a suite of software that expands beyond online surveys. The software scales across multiple modalities including web, phone, mobile (including mobile phones, kiosks, tablet PCs and PDAs), and paper. It supports all languages and the standard reporting services are provided in whichever language is used in the survey. Its online solution provides a comprehensive set of tools from basic survey questions in the study, to analytical tools sets in the analytic pack.

Its online questionnaire tool provides quite a bit of flexibility and customization. It is robust and has excellent integration capabilities with other software. It is relatively easy to move data in and out of its system.

The basic implementation of SnapSurveys is the Developer Tool. It is a PC-based developer system that renders the studies into a format that can be published online. The survey can be hosted over an internal web server or SnapSurveys will host it. As survey volume increases, SnapSurveys recommends purchasing a web-hosting tool to enable enhance features and handle large volumes. Other modules are available including reporting tools and monitoring tools. Snap-Surveys sells its software based on a developer licensing model, not a per completed survey model.

StatPac (www.statpac.com)

StatPac is sold in modules and by the number of licenses and service agreements you choose. It also offers a free trial that allows you to create a survey and collect 35 responses. With StatPac, you decide which analytical modules you want to purchase and its survey design module and data manager is included. The survey tool can handle scales, multiple- and single-response questions, open-ends and numeric text boxes, and can spell check in four languages. The basic statistical module provides crosstabs, banners, custom-designed statistical analysis, and graphics. Data can be downloaded to MS Word. The web survey module provides email list management capabilities and the ability to send email invites and reminders. StatPac also offers an advanced statistical module to perform advanced multivariate analytics such as multiple regressions, factor analysis, discriminate and cluster analysis. You can also create charts as part of the survey design and data manager module.

StatPac is a modular program that you can either download and deploy through your own servers or use via its hosting services. The Basics Statistics Module includes the functional capabilities that allow you to design the study, manage data, do basic statistical analysis, create graphics, and produce crosstabs. This module costs about what you would pay a full-service research company to run a set of tabs for one study. The Web Survey Module—which lets you design your study as well as manage your data, email lists, and upload and download data—is priced at about $500. The company also offers three months of free technical support and reasonable rates for on-demand technical support. A full year of technical support and maintenance can be purchased for a few hundred dollars. If all the modules are of interest, StatPac offers a combination that includes the basic statistical module, the web survey module, and a year of technical support for just under $1,000. The company also offers an Advanced Statistical Module for about $500 that allows you to perform multivariate analysis. The Additional Data Manager module, which is installed on multiple computers, allows simultaneous multiple data entry. This add-on goes for about $200 per user or just under $1,000 for unlimited users. StatPac also offers a perpetual license for ten users. It includes the basic analysis module, web survey module, advanced analysis module, and a year of technical support for a few thousand dollars.

SurveyGizmo (www.surveygizmo.com)

SurveyGizmo is online software with several packages. All versions of SurveyGizmo support over 20 question types including open-ends, ratings, grid questions with single and multiple responses, and numeric text boxes. There is also a question library. The survey tool can accommodate all languages, answer randomization, skip logic, piping, required questions, and images. You can modify the look and feel of the survey with customizable templates and font modifications. And like other survey tools, you can upload your logo.

In terms of analytics, the tool provides a summary report and data can be exported to Excel and .csv. The program also included graphic capabilities. At the higher-priced professional packages, you can create crosstabs and have access to a satisfaction meter and a TURF simulator.

SurveyGizmo offers the ability to send email invitations, reminders, and thank yous. However, it limits the number of survey invitations you can send out per month—its dedicated package allowing just 100,000 email invites per month. Depending on the quality of your list, participation rates and the number of surveys you run a month, you could burn through this invite cap pretty quickly.

SurveyGizmo has five packages beginning with a free package that allows for unlimited surveys and questions, 250 completes and one user. The Personal plan is less than $20 per month and allows for up to 1,000 completes per month. This is also a plan for one user and includes a few extras such as access to its question library and its email invitation system. SurveyGizmo's Pro package is less than $50 per month and like its other packages includes unlimited surveys and questions and up to 5,000 completes per month. Up to five users can use the Pro package, which includes extras found in the Personal package as well as more sophisticated programming capabilities such as piping and branching logic. At a few hundred dollars a month, the Enterprise package allows for up to 50,000 completes per month and 20 users. Private branding is also included. SurveyGizmo's top tier package is the Dedicated package at several hundred dollars a month. It includes up to a million completes per month and allows for up to 40 users.

Survey Methods (www.surveymethods.com)

Survey Methods focuses exclusively on online quantitative research spanning traditional survey research, including customer satisfaction, brand research, or product research. It has a comprehensive set of question types from single answer to multiple grid answer questions. However, the grid and scale questions do have some limitations based on length of the descriptor variable. Its target customer audience is companies conducting small- to mid-level research projects. It also provides an analytics toolset based on Microsoft Reporting Services. This provides basic reporting functionality of answer distribution and filtering by audience or other demographic information if needed.

Survey Methods' prices are some of the lowest in the industry. They charge based on a monthly subscription cost and incremental response volume for every additional 2,000 respondents. There are three tiers of pricing levels: Free/Basic, Advanced Package, and Professional package. The Basic package has the most limited functionality and only allows 500 completed surveys, but it is free. The Advanced package provides up to 1,000 completed surveys but has some limited functionality (listed at $9 per month). The Professional package provides the best value at $39 per month and 5,000 completed surveys. Additional completed surveys cost $5 per 2,000 completes. The feature set included in this package spans questionnaire design, fielding monitoring and reporting, and really provides the level of features required for at least a mid-level type study.

Vovici (www.vovici.com)

Vovici provides a full suite of online survey products and can cover just about any type of market research study. Its survey design tool is easy to use and provides the full spectrum of features needed for a survey platform. Most of its implementations are sold in a service model using the servers hosted at Vovici, but in some rare instances it will sell its software. Generally, highly sensitive initiatives conducted by government agencies (like the Department of Defense) require the software to be hosted internally.

Vovici offers two basic pricing packages: Professional and Enterprise. They are based on a combination of number of completed surveys as well as licensed survey users. The Professional version is considered the more basic version and is to be used for a more limited number of surveys per year. The entry price is reasonable, but it quickly goes up as the number of completed surveys and developer licenses increase. The Enterprise version is used for more wide-scale implementations.

Additional modules with advanced monitoring during the fielding process and advanced reporting features are available at extra cost. Vovici does not provide pricing online. Potential customers must submit an email online or call direct for pricing information.

Enterprise scalability

Though many mid-tier companies have software solutions for large companies, there are a few survey companies that can handle Enterprise class studies. The companies below can scale from small implementations to larger Enterprise implementations, but they are especially good in the mid-tier range and above.

Confirmit (www.confirmit.com)

Confirmit software is one of the biggest names in online survey tools and is often used by marketing research companies to power their surveys. It is one of the few companies that provides integration of multiple methodologies. It also has a tool that allows you to manage a community or panel. Confirmit offers training on how to maximize the use of its survey tool and through its learning center, it also provides free demos, downloads, and papers after completing a registration process. The company provides both a website version and a downloadable option. The survey tool has rich product features and functionality. To get more information on its capabilities, pricing, or to review its case studies, you must fill out a registration form with all your contact information and the company will contact you.

CustomerSat (www.customersat.com)

CustomerSat is actually the customer satisfaction survey tool provided by Market Tools. As a web-hosted software tool, this is an enterprise-based application that provides multi-channel survey delivery, meaning companies can survey across their business to reach customers, partners, employees, and prospects. The tool also provides guidelines on how to avoid over-surveying your constituents. The tool is able to handle large volumes of transactional customer satisfaction studies.

CustomerSat provides an analytics package that includes the ability to analyze comments and create loyalty indices. It also has the more common analytic tools such as crosstabs and significance testing. A chart designer is also part of the survey tool. One of the unique features of the survey tool is an "early warning system" functionality that allows you to see what accounts are potentially at risk. Other functionality the company promotes is the ability to customize how you interact with the data and how the data is displayed by way of widgets you drag and drop onto your homepage.

Since CustomerSat is primarily an enterprise application that provides both surveying capabilities and the ability to capture customer activities used to create its early warning system, this package is for large companies and can run into the hundreds of thousands of dollars. The parent company, Market Tools, does offer Market Tools Community Manager that includes both an online survey tool, called the Survey Manager and a panel management component so you can manage and develop your own panels. Contact the company for pricing that specifically addresses your needs.

Online Qualitative Research Tools

The following is a list of tool providers for online qualitative research.

Focus Vision (www.focusvision.com, 800-433-8128)

Focus Vision offers a product called InterVu. It is primarily a product for online focus groups. Its website says it can accommodate up to eight individuals. Focus Vision is well-known for its live video streaming capabilities and is extending online focus-group and message-board technology.

Software as a Service	Yes
Full-service online research	Yes
Online Message Boards	No
Online Focus Groups	Yes
Online One-on-One Interviews	Yes
Online Video Diaries	No
Cost per focus group	$900
Cost per 3-day message board	Not Available
Volume pricing	Yes
Tech support included with focus group	Yes
Tech support included with message board	Yes
Moderator view	Yes
Participant view	Yes
Client view	Yes
Supports images	Yes
Supports videos	Yes
Ability to download transcripts at the end of the board	Yes
Supports multiple languages	Yes
Ability for the moderator to take notes during the study and save for future use	Yes
A program management view to manage all research efforts	Yes

Itracks (www.itracks.com, 888-525-5026)

Itracks is one of the first companies to develop online solutions for hosting qualitative research. Their products cover focus groups, message boards, and one-on-one interviews. Itracks software is leased by many of the big research organizations.

Software as a Service	Yes
Full-service online research	Yes
Online Message Boards	Yes
Online Focus Groups	Yes
Online One-on-One Interviews	Yes
Online Video Diaries	Yes
Cost per focus group	$900
Cost per 3-day message board	$900
Volume pricing	Yes
Tech support included with focus group	Yes
Tech support included with message board	Yes
Moderator view	Yes
Participant view	Yes
Client view	Yes
Supports images	Yes
Supports videos	Yes
Ability to download transcripts at the end of the board	Yes
Supports multiple languages	Yes
Ability for the moderator to take notes during the study and save for future use	Yes
A program management view to manage all research efforts	Yes

Crusader Services (www.crusader-services.com, 323-871-2145)

Crusader Services offers an online focus group and message board tool. Although its website does not say it does one-on-one interviews, its tool appears capable of handling them.

Software as a Service	Yes
Full-service online research	Yes
Online Message Boards	Yes
Online Focus Groups	Yes
Online One-on-One Interviews	Yes
Online Video Diaries	No
Cost per focus group	$900
Cost per 3-day message board	$900
Volume pricing	Yes
Tech support included with focus group	Yes
Tech support included with message board	Yes
Moderator view	Yes
Participant view	Yes
Client view	Yes
Supports images	Yes
Supports videos	Yes
Ability to download transcripts at the end of the board	Yes
Supports multiple languages	Yes
Ability for the moderator to take notes during the study and save for future use	Yes
A program management view to manage all research efforts	Yes

artafact (www.artafact.com, 800-618-FACT)

Artafact is one of the leading providers of online qualitative research tools. The software is robust and the tool is easy to understand. It can be used for the three primary types of online qualitative research. The online focus group tool is based on web conferencing technology and the online message board tool is based on a social media platform. Artafact is also used by many of the leading research vendors.

Software as a Service	Yes
Full-service online research	Yes
Online Message Boards	Yes
Online Focus Groups	Yes
Online One-on-One Interviews	Yes
Online Video Diaries	Yes
Cost per focus group	$1,000
Cost per 3-day message board	$1,000
Volume pricing	Yes
Tech support included with focus group	Yes
Tech support included with message board	Yes
Moderator view	Yes
Participant view	Yes
Client view	Yes
Supports images	Yes
Supports videos	Yes
Ability to download transcripts at the end of the board	Yes
Supports multiple languages	Yes
Ability for the moderator to take notes during the study and save for future use	Yes
A program management view to manage all research efforts	Yes

E-focusgroups (www.e-focusgroups.com)

Probably the simplest design of all of the qualitative survey tools, e-focusgroups.com has a simple user tool to drive chat among focus-group participants. There is little preparation work with the board. A moderator types the questions into the board while the board is being conducted. Given that this platform is much like an instant message chat, the platform allows the moderator to completely change the guide on the fly. In other online message boards, the discussion guide has been preloaded and generally cannot be altered.

Software as a Service	Yes
Full-service online research	Yes
Online Message Boards	Yes
Online Focus Groups	Yes
Online One-on-One Interviews	Yes
Online Video Diaries	Yes
Cost per focus group	$500
Cost per 3-day message board	$700
Volume pricing	Yes
Tech support included with focus group	Yes
Tech support included with message board	Yes
Moderator view	Yes
Participant view	Yes
Client view	No
Supports images	Yes
Supports videos	Yes
Ability to download transcripts at the end of the board	Yes
Supports multiple languages	No
Ability for the moderator to take notes during the study and save for future use	Yes
A program management view to manage all research efforts	No

InsideHeads (insideheads.com, 877-In-Heads)

InsideHeads has recently released an online message board tool that can be serviced completely independently and with minimal training. Its program management view is especially helpful as it allows researchers to see across all of the projects that are being deployed. It appears to be the least expensive on the market, but it is also the newest. Its feature set is comparable to other top vendors including all of the high-end functionality like video and webcam support.

It is not set up for online message boards, but is actively building this tool.

Software as a Service	Yes
Full-service online research	Yes
Online Message Boards	No
Online Focus Groups	Yes
Online One-on-One Interviews	Yes
Online Video Diaries	No
Cost per focus group	$500
Cost per 3-day message board	$500
Volume pricing	Yes
Tech support included with focus group	Yes
Tech support included with message board	No
Moderator view	Yes
Participant view	Yes
Client view	Yes
Supports images	Yes
Supports videos	Yes
Ability to download transcripts at the end of the board	Yes
Supports multiple languages	Yes
Ability for the moderator to take notes during the study and save for future use	Yes
A program management view to manage all research efforts	Yes

YouGov Polimetrix (www.polimetrix.com, 800-998-6076)

YouGov Polimetrix has an online qualitative tool called VoxPop. Its unique selling position is that it integrates voice communication into the program in an organized fashion. Participants are put in a queue in order to participate in the discussion. The user interface is simple and quite easy to understand. Video and graphics can be integrated into the portal during the discussion. YouGov Polimetrix will fully service the research or also lease its software for independent use.

Software as a Service	Yes
Full-service online research	Yes
Online Message Boards	No
Online Focus Groups	Yes
Online One-on-One Interviews	No
Online Video Diaries	Yes
Cost per focus group	$500
Cost per 3-day message board	$500
Volume pricing	Yes
Tech support included with focus group	Yes
Tech support included with message board	No
Moderator view	Yes
Participant view	Yes
Client view	No
Supports images	Yes
Supports videos	Yes
Ability to download transcripts at the end of the board	Yes
Supports multiple languages	Yes
Ability for the moderator to take notes during the study and save for future use	Yes
A program management view to manage all research efforts	Yes

nqual (www.nqual.com, 44.20.7138.4057)

Nqual is based in the UK and has a nice suite of online qualitative products. It will partner with research vendors to license its products, but prefers to be a full research service. The online message board tool is called Powwow; the online focus group tool is called Rich Focus; and the online diary service is called MyLog. One-on-one interviews leverage the Rich Focus product. Its suite of products also includes social communities, ethnography, and a screener survey tool to help identify the right respondents for the research task at hand.

Software as a Service	Call for more information
Full-service online research	Yes
Online Message Boards	Yes
Online Focus Groups	Yes
Online One-on-One Interviews	Yes
Online Video Diaries	Yes
Cost per focus group	Call for quote
Cost per 3-day message board	Call for quote
Volume pricing	Yes
Tech support included with focus group	Yes
Tech support included with message board	Yes
Moderator view	Yes
Participant view	Yes
Client view	Yes
Supports images	Yes
Supports videos	Yes
Ability to download transcripts at the end of the board	Yes
Supports multiple languages	Yes
Ability for the moderator to take notes during the study and save for future use	Yes
A program management view to manage all research efforts	No

iModerate (www.imoderate.com, 303-333-7880)

iModerate has two qualitative products; Research>iMpact and Optimum!nsight. Optimum!nsight can be used as a focus group or one-on-one interviewing technology, conducted in real time. The solution provides the flexibility to conduct the study with either one participant or as many as the moderator can handle. Research>iMpact combines the use of a traditional quantitative survey with a qualitative survey. The respondents first engage in a quantitative study and their responses trigger a set of "why" questions for the moderator.